TAPAS

TAPAS

IRRESISTIBLE · SNACKS · FROM
S · P · A · I · N

A · D · R · I · A · N · L · I · N · S · S · E · N
W · I · T · H · S · A · R · A · C · L · E · A · R · Y

APPLE

A QUINTET BOOK

Published by Apple Press
Sheridan House
112-116A Western Road
Hove
East Sussex BN3 1DD

Reprinted 2001, 2002

ISBN 1-84092-255-9

This book was designed and produced by
Quintet Publishing Limited
6 Blundell Street
London N7 9BH

Creative Director: Peter Bridgewater
Art Director/Designer: Terry Jeavons
Editors: Caroline Beattie, Patricia Bayer
Photographer: Trevor Wood
Home Economy and Food Styling: Jonathan Higgins

Typeset in Great Britain by Central Southern Typesetters, Eastbourne
Manufactured in Hong Kong by Regent Publishing Services Ltd
Printed in Hong Kong by Midas Printing Limited

CONTENTS

INTRODUCTION   6

BASIC INGREDIENTS   11

SEAFOOD   13

VEGETABLES   43

EGG AND CHEESE   69

CHICKEN AND QUAIL   75

MEAT   83

INDEX   95

Assorted tapas in Seville

TAPAS are an integral part of the Spanish lifestyle. The tapas *bar is the focal point of every community; from the smallest village in Andalucia to Madrid and Barcelona. The easier communication between countries has brought about a cultural exchange which naturally includes the culinary arts; and the delights of tapas are now available far beyond Spanish borders.

Where and how tapas originated is disputed, but what is clear is that they have always been most frequently served with sherry, which is of course an Andalucian speciality. It appears that originally a slice of jamón serrano (cured ham) was served on a glass of sherry to keep the flies out; tapa is the Spanish word for cover or lid. Over a period of time the range of accompaniments was extended to the range available today throughout Spain.*

Córdoba's mezquita, a 16th-century church built within an eighth-century mosque

Tapas *are similar to appetizers or starters. However, they seem to remain ungoverned by the laws of their counterparts. They are unlimited by size, ingredient or*

Hungry shoppers waiting to buy chorizo and jamón serrano.

fixed sequence within a meal; and are therefore very difficult to define. The most useful description is that they are entire in themselves; in a larger form they may be served as meals, and in a smaller form as snacks. They may be liquid or solid: a soup is also a tapa; with or without a sauce, complex or simple, they involve the use of almost every ingredient from pulses and vegetables to fish and a host of meats, crustaceans, and shellfish. They present a wealth of choice, colour, smell and uninhibited experimentation – truly a chef's delight.

An awe-inspiring view from Ronda

Following hundreds of years of tradition the ritual of eating a tapa is part of every Spaniard's daily routine. From 11 o'clock in the morning everyone heads for his or her favourite bar for a chilled sherry, ice-cold beer and tapas, and, of course, conversation. This is repeated from 5pm till 9pm (or later) there are of course the usual meals through the day in addition to tapas.

A *good* tapas bar is an Aladdin's cave of indulgence. Ranged along the top of the bar stands an assortment of cheeses, prawns, crabs, scallops, chicken in garlic, prawns, tortilla, patatas bravas. From the ceiling are suspended the smoked serrano hams (cured in the Sierra Nevada), spiked in the base with a shafted metal cup to collect the oils. Stacked against the back wall are dusty bottles of red wine. By the early hours of the morning the floor will be littered with paper napkins, pips and crumbs. The informality and versatility of tapas cuisine makes eating it a sociable and relaxed experience.

The Giralda in Seville.
The palm trees provide a welcome refuge
from the midday heat.

The simple tapas such as chorizo sausage, stewed olives or anchovy and potato salad and others may be prepared in advance and refrigerated, to be served as a snack in between meals, with a glass of wine in the early evening or as a late supper. One of the more popular uses for tapas is as an appetizer before a main meal. Serve the marinated anchovies, the deep fried squid or goat's cheese in tarragon and garlic and these highly flavoured dishes will stimulate the palate while still leaving the room for something more substantial.

In warm weather, eating tapas-style will brighten up any picnic and add an extra touch of spontaneity to a barbecue — corn on the cob grilled with garlic butter, perhaps, or marinated lamb cutlets, brochettes, king prawns (giant shrimps) in garlic mayon-

A back street in Ronda

naise. For something rather more special, oysters Bloody Mary — or scallops with crab and lime. For the oysters just heat them sufficiently on the grill until they open, loosen from the shell, pour in the sauce and swallow — just keep the champagne close by!

Tapas are a delight for vegetarians as so many of the dishes do not include meats or their by-products. They can be served both as main dishes and side orders. Some favourites are patatas bravas, three peppers with tomato and garlic, green beans tapa or tortilla.

The more exotic and complicated tapas are ideally suited for special or celebratory occasions when presented as a main course. Bacon-wrapped prawns with sour cream, lobster and chicken brochettes, stuffed quail or the empanadas — the latter is a showstopper on arrival at the table.

A typical *tapas menu*

Slice open an empanada and the wonderful aromas of the filling will certainly put anticipatory smiles onto the faces of your friends. On a hot day what better than a ceviche, a lovely colourful chilled vegetable and prawn cocktail.

All the ingredients used in the recipes are easily obtainable and will suit all palates and all purses. Everything is adaptable, and these tapas are intended to suit every occasion.

The well-known and delicious calamares fritos

Hot or cold, large or small we hope that you will find something for everyone to enjoy both in the creation and the eating.

A bull-fight in Seville, with the Giralda in the background

10

BASIC INGREDIENTS
FOR THE RECIPES
IN THIS BOOK

GARLIC OIL or OILED GARLIC

This keeps well for a couple of weeks if covered and refrigerated. It is a good idea to have on hand if garlic is a favourite flavouring.

To flavour an olive oil, simply peel garlic cloves and marinate in the oil. An essential ingredient in many *tapas* recipes, however, is garlic oil, or oiled garlic. To make, peel any quantity of garlic – the amount of cloves or bulbs will depend on how much you expect to use within a couple of weeks. Heat the oven to about 230°C/450°F/Gas 7, place the whole bulbs on a tray and put in the hot oven for about 10 minutes. The garlic will pop out of its skin easily.

Crush the garlic in a food processor with enough olive oil to moisten. When it is a paste, the consistency of porridge, take out, cover, and refrigerate.

CHILLI OIL

This keeps indefinitely if refrigerated.

1¼ cups/250 ml/½ pt olive oil
6 red chillies, chopped

Heat the oil until hot and add the chillies. Cover and cook over low heat until the chillies turn black. Remove and cool. When cold, strain through a fine sieve, cover and refrigerate.

MAYONNAISE

Mayonnaise keeps well if it is covered and refrigerated. If you have never made it before, don't worry: it's very easy as long as you are aware of the following:

≈ Add the oil slowly; if the oil is warmed slightly, it reduces the risk of the sauce curdling.

≈ If during the making it becomes too thick, add a little vinegar or hot water.

≈ The sauce must be thoroughly whisked – the easiest way is to make it in a food processor or to use an electric whisk.

If your mayonnaise does curdle, however, you can bring it back by one of two methods:

≈ Take a clean bowl, add a dessertspoon of boiling water and gradually whisk in the curdled sauce, or

≈ The method I prefer: take another yolk, thinned with 5 ml/1 tsp cold water and whisked well, then gradually whisk into the curdled sauce.

For 1¼ cups/250 ml/½ pt mayonnaise:

2 egg yolks
10 ml/2 tsp vinegar
Salt and freshly ground black pepper
⅛ tsp mustard
1¼ cups/250 ml/½ pt olive oil
Approx 10 ml/2 tsp boiling water

≈ Place yolks, vinegar and seasoning in a bowl or food processor with the mustard.

≈ Gradually pour on the oil, very slowly, whisking or whizzing continually.

≈ Add the boiling water, whisking well.

≈ Correct the seasoning.

For garlic mayonnaise, add 1 tsp crushed garlic to the egg yolks for every 1¼ cups/250 ml/½ pt.

SHORTCRUST PASTRY

I like to make pastry by hand and for savoury tarts or pies I brush the sides of the bowl with garlic oil if I have any prepared in the refrigerator. It is also just as good made in a food processor.

For 400 g/1 lb shortcrust pastry:

400 g/1 lb plain flour
Pinch of salt and pepper
200 g/½ lb butter or margarine, softened slightly
3 egg yolks
A little cold water to bind

≈ Sieve (sift) the flour with the salt and pepper.
≈ Break the butter into small knobs and rub into the flour until it resembles breadcrumbs.
≈ Mix in the egg yolks.
≈ Add a few drops of cold water; this binds the pastry together and prevents it from becoming too sticky.
≈ Cover and refrigerate until it is needed.

CHICKEN STOCK

Although time-consuming, it is preferable, taste-wise, to make your own stock. I occasionally use stock (bouillon) cubes.

NOTE: These quantities may also be applied to a beef or veal stock.

1 kg/2 lb raw bones
10 cups/2 l/4 pt water
250 g/½ lb vegetables, such as onion, celery and leek, washed, peeled and roughly chopped
1 sprig of thyme
1 bay leaf
Parsley stalks
Handful of peppercorns

≈ Chop the bones, removing any fat.
≈ Place in a large pot, add the cold water and bring to the boil.
≈ Skim any scum from the top of the water, and simmer gently.
≈ Add the vegetables, herbs and peppercorns.
≈ Simmer for at least 3 hours.
≈ Skim, strain and either refrigerate for further use or use straightaway.
   Stocks will keep for 3–4 days in a refrigerator, and will also freeze well.

FISH STOCK

25 g/1 oz butter
1 kg/2 lb white fish bones, washed
250 g/½ lb vegetables, such as onion, celery and leek, peeled and roughly chopped
1 bay leaf
Juice of ½ lemon
Parsley stalks
6 peppercorns
10 cups/2 l/4 pt water

≈ Melt the butter in a large pan.
≈ Add the washed white fish bones, vegetables and flavourings to the pan.
≈ Cover and sweat for 5 minutes until the bones go transparent.
≈ Add the water, bring to the boil and skim. Simmer for 20 minutes, then strain.
≈ If the strained stock is put back on the heat and reduced by half its volume, the flavour is better.

MEDITERRANEAN VINAIGRETTE

To make this you will need the brine from an olive or gherkin jar.

Brine ⅔
Red wine vinegar ⅓
Olive oil ⅔
5 ml/1 tsp garlic per litre
15 ml/1 tbsp sugar per litre
15 ml/1 tbsp salt per litre
15 ml/1 tbsp black pepper per litre

≈ Mix together all the ingredients and leave to marinate for at least 30 minutes.

NOTE: The quantity of olive oil is the same as the quantities of red wine vinegar and brine together.

Seafood

14
PRAWNS (SHRIMPS) IN GARLIC

15
CHILLI KING PRAWNS
(GIANT SHRIMPS)

16
GLAZED KING PRAWNS
(GIANT SHRIMPS)

17
CEVICHE OF SHRIMP

18
KING PRAWN (GIANT SHRIMP) WITH
EGG AND ANCHOVY

BACON-WRAPPED PRAWNS (SHRIMPS)
WITH SOURED CREAM

19
PRAWNS (SHRIMPS) IN GARLIC
AND HERBS

MARINATED WHITEBAIT

20
DEEP-FRIED WHITEBAIT

21
CRAB AND BRANDY TARTLETS

LOBSTER AND CHICKEN BROCHETTES

22
FRIED SARDINES

23
SALT COD WITH GREEN PEPPERS
AND POTATOES

24
MONKFISH CULIACIN

MONKFISH WITH ANCHOVY SAUCE

26
MONKFISH WITH BACON BROCHETTES

27
SMOKED FISH MAYONNAISE AND
GARLIC TOAST

30
FISH CROQUETTES

GALICIAN STEWED OCTOPUS

31
OCTOPUS WITH OLIVE OIL AND
PAPRIKA

32
OYSTERS WITH LIME AND TABASCO

33
OYSTERS BLOODY MARY

34
SCALLOPS WITH LIME AND
SHREDDED CRAB

35
SCALLOPS IN TOMATO SAUCE

36
MUSSELS AND BEANS WITH TOMATO

37
SPINACH AND MUSSEL POT

38
ANCHOVY AND MUSSELS SAN
SEBASTIÁN

MUSSELS IN GAZPACHO

39
FRIED STUFFED MUSSELS

40
MUSSEL, SHRIMP AND SQUID TAPA

41
SQUID EMPANADA

42
FRIED SQUID

KING PRAWNS/GIANT SHRIMPS
IN GARLIC

INGREDIENTS

45ml/3tbsp olive oil

---

*12 king prawns (giant shrimps), fresh if available;
if not, cook from frozen*

2tsp garlic, crushed

2tsp paprika

30ml/2tbsp medium sherry

---

lemon wedges

PREPARATION

≈ Heat the oil in a pot. For frozen prawns (shrimps), lower heat, add the prawns (shrimps) to the oil, cover and cook for 6 minutes, until soft and heated through. For fresh, add to the oil until sizzling.

≈ Add the rest of the ingredients and bring to the boil. Taste for seasoning.

≈ Serve with lemon wedges.

CHILLI KING PRAWNS
(GIANT SHRIMPS)

INGREDIENTS

12 king prawns (giant shrimps), or ½kg/1lb monkfish, trimmed
and cut into 2cm/¾in cubes, or ½kg/1lb scampi

INGREDIENTS FOR THE MARINADE

2tsp garlic, crushed

1½ cups/375ml/12 fl oz groundnut oil

6 red chillies, seeded and chopped

salt and black pepper (¼tsp each)

PREPARATION

≈ Blend together all the above ingredients in a food
processor. Pour this over the prawns (shrimps) and
leave for 4 hours.

≈ Remove the prawns (shrimps) and grill (broil), or
sauté in melted butter. Keep the marinade.

INGREDIENTS FOR THE SAUCE

75g/3oz butter (preferably unsalted), melted

juice of 4 juicy lemons

PREPARATION

≈ Melt the butter and whisk in the lemon juice.
≈ Add 90ml/6tbsp of the marinade.
≈ Bring to the boil, pour over the prawns and serve.

15

GLAZED KING PRAWNS
(GIANT SHRIMPS)

INGREDIENTS

12 king prawns (giant shrimps); if frozen, defrost

2 egg yolks

1¼ cups/250ml/½pt mayonnaise (see Basic Recipe)

15ml/1tbsp double (heavy) cream

black pepper

½tsp paprika

1 tomato, skinned and chopped into small squares

3tsp garlic, crushed

1tbsp parsley, chopped

PREPARATION

≈ Carefully remove the shell from the tails of the prawns (shrimps), keeping the heads intact.

≈ Whisk the yolks into the mayonnaise with the double (heavy) cream, black pepper, paprika, tomato and garlic.

≈ Heat the grill (broiler).

≈ Brush a baking sheet with oil.

≈ Place the prawns (shrimps) on the baking sheet and spoon the mayonnaise mixture over the tails.

≈ Heat under the grill until brown spots appear.

≈ Sprinkle the prawns (shrimps) with chopped parsley and serve immediately with lemon or lime wedges and garlic bread.

CEVICHE OF SHRIMP

INGREDIENTS

1 kg / 2 lb shrimps or prawns, or ½ kg / 1 lb shrimps and ½ kg / 1 lb white fish, skinned and cleaned

5 cups / 1 ½ pt water

2 ½ cups / ½ l / 1 pt lime juice

2 red onions, chopped

30 ml / 2 tbsp soy sauce

salt and pepper

2 cucumbers, seeded, skinned, halved lengthwise and cut into half moons

1 red pepper, seeded and thinly sliced

1 bunch of dill, chopped

tabasco sauce to taste

lime wedges to garnish

PREPARATION

≈ Place the prawns or shrimps in a large bowl.

≈ Mix the ingredients for the marinade together (water, lime juice, red onions, soy sauce, salt and pepper) and pour over the prawns or shrimps.

≈ Marinate for 20 minutes.

≈ Add the cucumber, pepper slices and dill. Toss.

≈ Spoon onto plates or into small bowls.

≈ Sprinkle with pepper and tabasco sauce. Serve with lime wedges.

KING PRAWNS (GIANT SHRIMPS) WITH EGG AND ANCHOVY

You need 6 cocktail sticks for this recipe.

INGREDIENTS

6 king prawns (giant shrimps), peeled
(it is optional to remove the heads)

3 hard-boiled eggs, shelled and halved

6 anchovy fillets

6 black olives

150ml/ ¼pt mayonnaise (see Basic Recipes)

PREPARATION

≈ On each stick, spear 1 prawn (shrimp) tail, half a boiled egg, a rolled anchovy fillet and a black olive. Either cover in mayonnaise, or serve as a dip.

BACON-WRAPPED PRAWNS (SHRIMPS) WITH SOURED CREAM

This is a lovely tapa, and a very popular barbecue snack.

INGREDIENTS

12 giant prawns (shrimps), shelled, leaving on the head and tail tip (defrost overnight if using frozen)

½ cup/ 100g/ 4oz grated fresh mozzarella cheese

1tsp freshly ground black pepper

12 slices good bacon, trimmed of the rind and excess fat

a little olive oil

PREPARATION

≈ Make a slit lengthwise along the back of the prawns (shrimps), but do not cut through.
≈ Fill the slit with the cheese, mixed with the black pepper.
≈ Wrap each prawn (shrimp) in one rasher (strip) of bacon, starting at the head, which should peep out, and slightly spiral the bacon to the tail.
≈ Paint with olive oil, and either grill (broil) or bake in a hot oven, 230°C/450°F/gas 8, for 7–10 minutes. Meanwhile, prepare the dip.

INGREDIENTS FOR THE SAUCE/DIP

1 cup/ 200g/ 8oz soured cream

½tsp each salt and black pepper

juice of ½ lemon

TO PREPARE THE SAUCE/DIP

≈ Mix all the ingredients together for the sauce, and serve with the hot prawns (shrimps).

PRAWNS (SHRIMPS) IN GARLIC AND HERBS

INGREDIENTS

1¼ cups/250ml/½pt olive oil

½kg/1lb prawns (shrimps), peeled; if using frozen, cook

2tbsp garlic, crushed

1½tbsp parsley, chopped

1½tbsp coriander, chopped

salt and freshly ground black pepper

3 lemons, cut into wedges

PREPARATION

≈ Heat the oil in a pot.

≈ Add the prawns (shrimps), cover, lower heat and cook for 2 minutes, until the heat goes through them.

≈ Add the garlic, herbs, salt and freshly ground pepper.

≈ Stir and cook for a further 2 minutes.

≈ Serve in small bowls with lemon wedges.

MARINATED WHITEBAIT

INGREDIENTS

½kg/1lb bag of frozen whitebait, defrosted (for about 2 hours at room temperature)

1tbsp parsley, chopped

2tsp garlic, crushed

2tsp freshly ground black pepper

juice of 2 lemons (or enough to cover the fish while they marinate)

2 shallots, finely chopped

1tsp freshly ground black pepper

½tsp salt

60ml/4tbsp olive oil

PREPARATION

≈ Remove heads of whitebait. Split lengthwise for the larger ones, leave the small ones whole. Pull out the bone of the larger ones.

≈ Place on a tray or in a square dish (not a metal dish).

≈ Cover with parsley, garlic, lemon juice, shallots and seasoning.

≈ Leave to marinate for 24 hours in the refrigerator.

≈ Drain off the excess juice.

≈ Cover with the oil, leave for 1 hour and then serve.

DEEP-FRIED WHITEBAIT

INGREDIENTS

½kg/1lb frozen whitebait

½ cup/120ml/4fl oz milk, at room temperature

flour to coat

oil

salt, preferably sea salt

6 lemon wedges

PREPARATION

≈ Shake the frozen whitebait into the milk. If the milk is too cold, small ice particles will form; if this happens, add a few drops of hot water.

≈ Shake the whitebait thoroughly into flour. Toss thoroughly in a sieve to remove excess flour.

≈ Place in a frying basket.

≈ Fry in hot oil for 3 minutes in 2 or 3 batches; too many together will stick in the basket.

≈ Sprinkle with salt and serve immediately with lemon wedges.

CRAB AND BRANDY TARTLETS

For 6 tartlets or one 20cm/8in flan ring:

INGREDIENTS

200g/½lb shortcrust pastry (see Basic Recipes)

50g/2oz butter

½ medium onion, finely chopped (preferably a red onion, as the flavour is milder)

1 tsp tomato paste

pinch of sugar

½ glass of white wine

½kg/1lb crabmeat

pinch of nutmeg

1 tbsp parsley, chopped

salt and freshly ground black pepper

juice of 2 oranges

1 shot of brandy (about ⅛ cup/1oz)

4 eggs (size 3) and 1 extra yolk

1¼ cups/250ml/½pt milk (or, for a richer flavour, use the same amount of single (light) cream)

⅔ cup/75g/3oz manchego cheese

PREPARATION

≈ Prepare the pastry, rest it and line the moulds thinly. Bake blind: cover the pastry with tin foil, fill the case with beans and cook in a hot oven (230°C/450°F/gas 7) for 5–8 minutes.

TO PREPARE THE FILLING

≈ In a saucepan, melt the butter. Add the onion and cover. Cook gently until the onion is soft.

≈ Add the tomato paste and sugar, then the white wine.

≈ Stir in the crabmeat, nutmeg, parsley, salt and pepper.

≈ Add the orange juice and brandy, simmer gently for 5 minutes. Stir and remove. Cool.

≈ Make a custard: in a large bowl, blend the eggs with the milk or cream, whisking well.

≈ Mix the crab mixture and manchego into the custard, check the seasoning, and add some freshly ground black pepper.

≈ Spoon the crab mixture into the pastry moulds or flan ring.

≈ Bake in a moderate oven (180°C/350°F/gas 4) until golden-brown and set, for approximately 15–20 minutes.

LOBSTER AND CHICKEN BROCHETTES

You will need 6 skewers for this recipe.

INGREDIENTS

2 live lobsters, each ¾kg/1½lb

2 chicken breasts, each 200g/8oz, cubed into bite-sized pieces

dry white wine

2 limes, peeled and cut into segments

½ cup/120ml/¼pt garlic and tomato mayonnaise (see Basic Recipe; to this add half its volume plum tomatoes, canned, and mix all in a food processor, adding more salt, pepper and plenty of garlic – 2tsp for every 1¼ cups/250ml/½pt mayonnaise)

PREPARATION

≈ Place the lobsters in a pot of boiling salted water. Lower heat and simmer for 5 minutes, or until they go pink.

≈ Pull the tail section away from the head with a little twist. Remove the shells and cut the flesh into chunks.

≈ Poach the chicken pieces in a little white wine for 6–8 minutes. Cool.

≈ Arrange the lobster, chicken and lime segments alternately on sticks.

≈ Coat with the tomato and garlic mayonnaise.

FRIED SARDINES

INGREDIENTS

12 sardines (about 10cm/4in long)

½ cup/50g/2oz seasoned flour

INGREDIENTS FOR THE MARINADE, BLEND TOGETHER:

2tsp parsley, chopped

60ml/4tbsp lemon juice

½tsp garlic, crushed

salt and black pepper

60ml/4tbsp olive oil

PREPARATION

≈ Take the sardines (if the head is on, leave it) and cut through the bellies lengthwise without cutting through the bone. Butterfly the fish.

≈ Paint the marinade on the fish, and leave for 20 minutes.

≈ Shake the flour over the fish, dusting until well-covered. Shake off any excess flour. Season.

≈ Heat the oil until hot and fry the sardines, turning to brown both sides.

INGREDIENTS FOR THE SAUCE/DIP

salt and black pepper to taste

1 beef (large) tomato, skinned and chopped

1 small green pepper, seeded and chopped

25g/1oz onion, chopped

enough mayonnaise (see Basic Recipes), to bind

TO PREPARE THE SAUCE/DIP

≈ Mix all the ingredients together, then either spoon onto plates with the sardines, or use as a dip.

SALT COD WITH GREEN PEPPERS AND POTATOES

INGREDIENTS

¾kg/1½lb dried salt cod, chopped into bite-sized pieces

20ml/2tbsp olive oil

1 large onion, chopped

1 celery stalk, chopped

1 medium green pepper, seeded and finely sliced

1 large leek, washed and chopped

1 tsp garlic, crushed

4 medium potatoes, washed and sliced into
1.25cm/½in-thick rounds

1 glass of dry white wine

1½ cups/330ml/⅔pt fish stock (see Basic recipes)

black pepper

1 tbsp parsley, chopped

PREPARATION

≈ Soak the salt cod for 24 hours, with at least 3 changes of water. Cut into 5cm/2in pieces.

≈ Heat the oil in a pot, and gently cook the onion, celery and green pepper.

≈ Add the leek, garlic, potato and wine. Reduce the wine by one-half.

≈ Add the stock, cover with a lid and simmer until the vegetables are soft. You may need a bit more liquid; if so, add a little water.

≈ Add the cod and plenty of black pepper. Stir and cook for a further 6–8 minutes.

≈ Serve the fish in shallow bowls, with plenty of sauce and chopped parsley.

MONKFISH WITH ANCHOVY SAUCE

INGREDIENTS

½kg/1lb monkfish tail, skinned, cleaned and cubed

flour

½ cup/120ml/4fl oz olive oil

¼ cup/60ml/2fl oz anchovy essence

1 tbsp ground black pepper

PREPARATION

≈ Season the fish and lightly dust with flour.

≈ Heat the oil in a pan, add monkfish pieces and lower heat.

≈ Cover and cook for 4–6 minutes, until the flesh is still quite springy and very slightly underdone.

≈ Remove from the sauce and keep warm.

≈ Add the rest of the ingredients to the pan and bring to the boil.

≈ Taste for a strong sharp peppery flavour.

≈ Return the fish to the sauce, stir and serve.

MONKFISH CULIACIN

For this recipe, you need six large skewers.

INGREDIENTS

1kg/2lb monkfish tail, skinned, boned and cubed; marinate in liquid (3 parts water to 1 part lime juice)

INGREDIENTS FOR THE SAUCE

4 red chillies, seeded and chopped

olive oil

2 beef (large) tomatoes, peeled and chopped

1 tsp oregano

1 tsp black pepper

1 tsp cumin seed

1 tsp ground ginger

2tsp garlic

2½ cups/½l/1pt fish stock (see Basic Recipes)

½ large cucumber

1 red onion

lime wedges

tabasco sauce to taste

PREPARATION

≈ Fry the chilli in a little olive oil, until dark.

≈ Blend together the chopped tomato, oregano, black pepper, cumin seed, garlic and fish stock. Add to the chillies.

≈ Bring to the boil and simmer for 10 minutes. Remove from heat

≈ Cut the cucumber into .6-cm/¼-in rounds.

≈ Cut the red onion into eighths, by halving like an orange, then quartering each half.

≈ Make up the skewers, by piercing a piece of onion, a piece of fish, a piece of cucumber, etc., until the skewer is full.

≈ Coat liberally with the sauce.

≈ Serve with lime wedges and tabasco sauce.

MONKFISH AND BACON BROCHETTES

You need 6 skewers or 12 smaller sticks for this recipe.

INGREDIENTS

24 *small button mushrooms*

9 *slices good bacon, sliced in 7.5cm/3in lengths*

½*kg/1lb monkfish tail, boned, skinned and cubed into small chunks*

olive oil

salt and pepper

½ *cup/120ml/¼pt tomato and garlic mayonnaise (see Basic Recipes) with half the volume of canned tomatoes whisked in*

PREPARATION

≈ Start by piercing a mushroom on the skewer, then add a piece of folded bacon, then a piece of fish. Repeat until the stick is full and all the ingredients (or sticks) are used up.

≈ Brush with olive oil and season. At this stage you may keep in the refrigerator until needed.

≈ Cook by placing on an oiled tray in a hot oven (220°C/425°F/gas 7) for approximately 7–8 minutes, until cooked.

≈ Dredge with mayonnaise and serve.

SMOKED FISH MAYONNAISE AND GARLIC TOAST

This is a lovely tapa.

INGREDIENTS

2 green peppers, deseeded and cut into thin strips

60ml/4tbsp olive oil

black pepper

1 tomato, peeled and chopped

200g/½lb smoked mackerel

200g/½lb smoked cod (you could use cooked salt cod, but if you do, eliminate salt from the seasoning)

½ cup/100g 120ml/4oz garlic mayonnaise (see Basic Recipes)

6 slices of bread, cut into triangles, or 1 French stick, cut in rounds

5g garlic, crushed

30ml/2tbsp olive oil

PREPARATION

≈ Stew the peppers over a low heat in the oil, add black pepper and the tomato. Cover and stew for 20 minutes, or until soft. Cool.

≈ Skin and bone the fish, mix the mayonnaise into it and blend in a food processor with black pepper. It should reach double (heavy) cream consistency; add more garlic mayonnaise if necessary.

≈ Brush the bread on both sides with the garlic and 30ml/2tbsp olive oil. Bake in the oven until golden.

≈ Spoon a little of the pepper mixture over the bread toasties.

≈ Spoon some smoked fish mix on to the pepper and serve — Spanish club sandwich style!

Sunset shows up the vibrant colours of Córdoba and the Guadalquivir River (a great source of inspiration for writers of flamenco music and songs). A past fought over by Moors, Jews and Christians is still evident in the architecture but life these days is much more tranquil.

FISH CROQUETTES

INGREDIENTS

300g/12oz white fish; wash, half-cover with milk and poach in the oven for 15 minutes. Remove all skin, bone and flake the fish.

1½ cups/300g/12oz mashed potatoes

¼ cup/50g/2oz onion, chopped

butter

½tsp garlic, crushed

½tsp paprika

1 tbsp parsley, chopped

1 egg

eggwash (2 eggs and a little milk)

¼ cup/50g/2oz flour

white breadcrumbs

PREPARATION

≈ Prepare the fish.

≈ Prepare the mashed potatoes (both can be prepared in advance).

≈ Soften the onion in a little butter, add the garlic, paprika and parsley. Stir, and remove from the heat.

≈ Mix the fish, potatoes and onion together, blending well, and season.

≈ Beat in the egg. The resulting mixture should be firm and pliable.

≈ Form the mix into little balls.

≈ Cover with flour, shake off any excess and pass through the eggwash to cover completely.

≈ Pass through the breadcrumbs.

≈ Reshape if necessary.

≈ These may be deep-fried in hot oil (185°C/365°F) for 3–5 minutes until golden, or shallow-fried in melted butter, shaking the pan to brown evenly.

≈ Serve with tomato and garlic mayonnaise (see recipe for Lamb and Chicken Brochettes) and lemon wedges.

GALICIAN STEWED OCTOPUS

INGREDIENTS

1 2–3kg/4–6lb octopus

45ml/3tbsp white wine vinegar

2 onions, chopped

1 tbsp garlic, crushed

1 bay leaf

15 peppercorns

plenty of paprika

sea salt

PREPARATION

≈ Clean the octopus:
Cut the legs off just below the eye. Push the beak out through the centre of the legs with your finger.
Cut the eyes off the body and discard.
Turn the body inside out, discard guts and rinse out.
Cut the tentacles into 3.8-cm/1½-in pieces, discarding any small ends.
Chop the body sac into similar mouth-sized pieces.

≈ Cover the octopus with cold water in a pot, cover and bring to the boil. Remove and plunge into cold water. Bring to the boil again, cool and repeat. This time add the vinegar, onion, garlic and herbs.

≈ Simmer until the octopus is tender, for approximately 20 minutes. Test frequently as there is a period of time when the octopus goes from chewy to tender and back to chewy again.

≈ Sprinkle liberally with paprika and sea salt, and serve on a large plate (in Spain, wooden boards are used).

OCTOPUS WITH OLIVE OIL AND PAPRIKA

Don't be put off by the amount of oil in this recipe, which is delicious with chunks of fresh bread.

INGREDIENTS

one 2–3kg/4–6lb octopus

olive oil to cover

2tbsp paprika

2tbsp garlic, crushed

½tbsp salt

PREPARATION

≈ Prepare the octopus as for Galician Stewed Octopus; drain from the cooking liquid and chop into bite-sized pieces.

≈ Cover the octopus with olive oil.

≈ Add the paprika, garlic and salt to the oil.

≈ Bring to the boil and cook for 2 minutes. Remove from the heat and cool, or else serve immediately.

This dish will keep in the refrigerator for 2–3 days. It may be microwaved if covered with plastic film. The secret to the sauce here is the salt, which counteracts the blandness created by so much oil.

OYSTERS WITH LIME AND TABASCO

INGREDIENTS

12 *large fresh oysters*

tabasco sauce

juice of 4 limes

freshly ground black pepper

PREPARATION

≈ Open the oysters carefully.

≈ Add 2 drops of tabasco sauce to each one.

≈ Sprinkle with lime juice and black pepper.

≈ Swallow.

OYSTERS BLOODY MARY

INGREDIENTS

12 oysters

vodka

tabasco sauce

Worcestershire sauce

salt and pepper

lemon juice

cucumber, peeled and finely chopped

celery stalks (small, young ones)

tomato juice

PREPARATION

≈ Mix a spicy Bloody Mary using all the above ingredients except for the oysters; mix in a blender with some ice cubes so it is well-chilled.

≈ Open the oysters carefully and fill the shells with the Bloody Mary mix.

≈ If there's any left over, drink it!

SCALLOPS WITH LIME AND CRAB

INGREDIENTS

12 small to medium, or 6 large scallops
(slice the latter across horizontally)

juice of 4 limes

juice of 2 oranges

1 shot of brandy

1 small piece of root ginger, grated

salt and pepper

1 cup/200g/½lb white crab meat

PREPARATION

≈ Open the scallops. Trim away the muscular 'foot'. Wash and place in the refrigerator, in the cleaned shells, on a tray.

≈ Mix the lime juice, orange juice, brandy, ginger and seasoning together and spoon over the scallops.

≈ Marinate for 4–6 hours. The scallops will go opaque and be firm to the touch when ready.

≈ Lightly season the crab meat and flake over the scallops.

≈ Serve well chilled.

SCALLOPS IN TOMATO SAUCE

This tapa is like a mini-meal.

INGREDIENTS

12 small or 6 large scallops

50g/2oz butter

1 glass of dry white wine

INGREDIENTS FOR THE SAUCE

50g/2oz butter

¼ cup/50g/2oz flour

2½ cups/500ml/1pt milk, warmed

½tbsp tomato paste

1 tsp garlic, crushed

1 tsp sugar

2 beef (large) tomatoes, peeled and finely chopped

15ml/1tbsp double (heavy) cream

½tsp black pepper

½ cup/100g/4oz grated Parmesan cheese

INGREDIENTS FOR THE POTATO

1kg/2lb potatoes

salt

⅔ cup/75g/3oz butter

2 egg yolks

salt and pepper

30ml/2tbsp single (light) cream, warmed

2tsp parsley, chopped

PREPARATION

≈ Prepare the scallops: Open by placing in the oven at 230°C/450°F/gas 8 for a few minutes. Cut the scallop with a sharp knife, trim off the root and wash well.

≈ Wash the shells and keep to one side.

≈ Separate the pink coral from the white of the scallop and keep in the refrigerator.

≈ Prepare the sauce: Melt the butter, stir in the flour and cook to a sandy texture.

≈ Gradually whisk in the warmed milk.

≈ Whisk in the tomato paste, the garlic and the sugar.

≈ Stir occasionally and simmer for 20 minutes to cook out the flour. Stir in the chopped tomatoes, cream, cheese and pepper. Keep to one side until needed.

≈ While the sauce is cooking, prepare the mashed potato. Peel, wash and chop the potatoes into even pieces, place in salted water, bring to the boil and cook until soft.

≈ Drain the potatoes thoroughly, return to the pot, cover and place over a low heat, shaking occasionally to dry out the potatoes.

≈ Mash with 25g/1oz butter.

≈ With a wooden spoon, mix in the yolks and the rest of the butter. Beat in the warm cream and season well. Stir in the chopped parsley.

≈ Take a piping bag, with a star nozzle, and fill with the potato.

≈ Cook the scallops: Melt the butter and when hot, toss in the scallops (keeping the pink corals back, as they take less cooking). Seal both sides.

≈ Add the wine, bring to the boil, add the pink corals and simmer for 3 minutes.

≈ Place the shells on a baking tray, and spoon 1tsp of sauce into each shell.

≈ Replace a scallop and a coral into each shell. Spoon the sauce over.

≈ Pipe the potato in little stars around the edge of the shell.

≈ Sprinkle the cheese over and place in a hot oven, 220°C/425°F/gas 7, for 5 minutes or until cheese is browned. Serve with lemon wedges.

MUSSELS AND BEANS WITH TOMATO

INGREDIENTS

1kg/2lb haricot (white navy) beans

30ml/2tbsp olive oil

1 onion, chopped

2 slices good bacon, chopped

2tsp garlic, crushed

5 cups/1½pt chicken stock (see Basic Recipes)

1kg/2lb mussels, washed and debearded

1 beef (large) tomato, peeled and chopped

1tbsp parsley, chopped

juice of 1 lemon

salt and pepper

PREPARATION

≈ Soak the beans overnight in cold water, or buy ready-to-cook beans.

≈ Heat the oil and sweat the onion in it until soft. Add the bacon and stir.

≈ Add the beans and garlic, cover with the chicken stock and cook (20 minutes for canned beans, 2 hours for dried, soaked beans).

≈ Add the mussels, shake, cover and cook until the mussels open.

≈ Stir in the tomato, parsley and lemon juice. Season and serve in small bowls.

SPINACH AND MUSSEL POT

INGREDIENTS

½kg/1lb spinach

1 onion, chopped

50g/2oz butter

1 tsp garlic, crushed

pinch of nutmeg

salt and black pepper

1 glass of dry white wine

3 ¾ cups/¾l/1½pt chicken stock (see Basic Recipes)

1kg/2lb mussels, cleaned and debearded

30ml/2tbsp single (light) cream

PREPARATION

≈ If using fresh spinach, pick it over and discard any stalks and large veins. Wash thoroughly. Note: It is only necessary to cook fresh spinach.

≈ Place the spinach in boiling salted water. Boil for 2 minutes. Remove and cool under the cold tap. Squeeze to remove all moisture. Chop finely.

≈ Sweat the onion in the butter. Add the spinach, garlic, nutmeg, salt and black pepper.

≈ Add the white wine and turn up the heat. Cook for 5 minutes, until the wine is almost dry.

≈ Add the stock and bring to the boil. Stir and cook for 5 minutes.

≈ The consistency should be that of double (heavy) cream; if it's too thin, continue cooking over heat, stirring.

≈ Add the mussels and cover the pot. Cook until the mussels have opened, continuously shaking the pot.

≈ Remove from heat and taste for seasoning. Ground black pepper will highlight the spinach flavour.

≈ Pour into bowls, evenly distributing the mussels. Swirl a little cream over each and serve.

ANCHOVY AND MUSSELS SAN SEBASTIÁN

INGREDIENTS

2 medium onions, chopped

2 green peppers, seeded and finely chopped

½ cup/120ml/4fl oz olive oil

1 tsp garlic, crushed

1 tbsp paprika

½kg/1lb anchovies, fresh, or ½kg/1lb whitebait, frozen, defrosted

1 cup/240ml/8fl oz dry white wine

1 cup/240ml/8fl oz vinegar

1¼ cups/240ml/½pt fish stock (see Basic Recipes)

1kg/2lb mussels, cleaned and debearded

PREPARATION

≈ Sweat the onions and peppers in the olive oil.

≈ Add the garlic and paprika, stir and add the fish.

≈ Simmer for approximately 5 minutes.

≈ Pour on the wine, vinegar and stock, and bring to the boil.

≈ Add the mussels. Cover and cook, until the mussels open.

≈ Season and serve in shallow dishes.

MUSSELS IN GAZPACHO

INGREDIENTS

½ medium onion, finely chopped

1¼ cups/250ml/½pt dry white wine

2 parsley stalks

piece of lemon rind

1kg/2lb mussels, cleaned, debearded and any open ones discarded

5 cups/1½pt gazpacho (see recipe), chilled;
add more vinegar and black pepper to make spicier and tarter

PREPARATION

≈ Place onion, wine, parsley and lemon rind in a saucepan and bring to the boil.

≈ Pour in the mussels. Cover, shake and cook until open.

≈ Remove pan from heat and cool.

≈ When cold, pour in the *gazpacho*, stir and spoon into bowls.

≈ Serve with crusty bread and preferably garlic butter.

FRIED STUFFED MUSSELS

INGREDIENTS

1 medium onion, chopped

50g/2oz butter

1¼ cups/250ml/½pt dry white wine

2 parsley stalks

a shaving of lemon rind

36 mussels (about 1kg/2lb), cleaned, debearded and any open ones discarded

1¼ cups/250ml/¼pt béchamel sauce made with 75g/3oz butter, ⅔ cup/75g/3oz flour, and salt and pepper (see below)

125g/5oz raw ham (Spanish jamón serrano or Italian prosciutto or Parma ham would be suitable)

1 cup/200g/7oz soft white breadcrumbs

⅔ cup/75g/3oz grated Parmesan cheese

salt and pepper

4 eggs, beaten with ¼ cup warm water

oil for frying

2tbsp parsley, chopped

PREPARATION

≈ Sweat the onion in butter in a pot.

≈ Add the wine, parsley stalks, lemon rind and bring to the boil.

≈ Add the mussels, cover and shake pot over high heat until the shells open.

≈ Remove the mussels with a slotted spoon and place in a bowl to cool.

≈ Strain the cooking liquid and keep it to add to the béchamel.

≈ Make the béchamel:
Melt the butter; stir in the flour.
Warm 1¼ cups/250ml/½pt milk and add gradually, beating with a wooden spoon.
Add the mussel liquid and simmer for 20 minutes. Season.
The béchamel sauce should be quite thick.

≈ Remove the mussels from the shells (keeping the shells to one side).

≈ Mince (grind) the mussels with the ham and with a teaspoon put back into the shells, leaving space for the sauce.

≈ Spread the béchamel over with a spoon or small palette knife. The béchamel will seal the mixture. Refrigerate until firm, approximately 1 hour.

≈ Mix the breadcrumbs with the cheese and season.

≈ Dip the mussels in the egg dip, then in the crumbs, until evenly coated.

≈ Shallow-fry in hot oil.

≈ Drain on greaseproof paper and serve immediately, garnished with parsley.

39

MUSSEL, SHRIMP AND SQUID TAPA

INGREDIENTS

7½ cups/1½l/3pt olive oil

½kg/1lb prawns (shrimps) in shell, frozen

3¾ cups/¾l/1½pt lemon juice

1kg/2lb mussels, cleaned, debearded and any open ones discarded

½kg/1lb squid, cleaned (as in recipe for Fried Squid) and blanched

3tsp garlic, crushed

3tsp paprika

salt and pepper

PREPARATION

≈ In a saucepan, bring the oil to the boil and add the prawns (shrimps). Cover and take off the heat. Leave for 3 minutes to heat the prawns (shrimps) through.

≈ Add the rest of the ingredients, return to heat and bring to the boil.

≈ Cover, shake until the mussels open.

≈ Season and serve in small bowls.

SQUID EMPANADA

An empanada is a Spanish pie which can have a variety of fillings. It can be bound in a shortcrust, a bread dough or even a puff pastry made with lard. Individual ones are sometimes made, although it is more usual to bake a large one in a paella pan and serve it cold in slices — a delicious centrepiece to any tapas display.

INGREDIENTS FOR THE FILLING

60ml/4tbsp olive oil

100g/4oz onion, chopped

1 tsp garlic, crushed

2 green peppers, seeded and cut into fine strips

3 tomatoes, peeled and halved

2 red chillies, seeded and chopped

½kg/1lb squid, prepared as in recipe for Fried Squid, first 9 steps

1 cup/240ml/8fl oz red Rioja wine

1 cup/240ml/8fl oz fish stock (see Basic Recipes)

1–2tsp salt

2tsp paprika

Sprig of fresh thyme

½kg/1lb mussels, cleaned, debearded and simmered in a little boiling salted water for 5 minutes

1 cup/200g/½lb peeled prawns

salt and pepper

2¼ cups/450g/18oz yeast dough

2 tomatoes, sliced and peeled

1 egg yolk mixed with a little milk to glaze the pie

PREPARATION

≈ Heat the oil in a large frying pan and gently cook the onion and garlic. Add the peppers and tomatoes.

≈ Add the chillies, stir and cook for 10 minutes.

≈ Add the rings of squid, with the chopped legs.

≈ Pour in the red wine and stock, cover and cook for 20 minutes over a moderate heat. Add the salt, paprika and thyme; stir. If the mixture looks a little dry, add some water.

≈ Remove the mussels from the shells and add to the mixture along with the prawns (shrimps). Remove from heat and season.

INGREDIENTS FOR THE DOUGH

2¼ cups/450g/18oz plain flour

generous ⅛ cup/25g/1oz fresh yeast (or ¹⁄₁₆ cup/12.5g/ ½oz dried yeast)

270ml/9fl oz milk, lukewarm

50g/2oz butter

2 eggs · 1 tsp salt

PREPARATION

≈ Sieve (sift) the flour into a bowl and make a well in the centre.

≈ Crumble or sprinkle the yeast into the well. Pour in the lukewarm milk and stir to dissolve the yeast. Cover with a fine layer of flour. Do not blend this in.

≈ Cover the bowl with a cloth and leave the mixture to rise for 15 minutes in a warm place. When the yeast has risen enough, cracks in the covering layer of flour will appear.

≈ While the mixture is rising, melt the butter in a pan, add the eggs and beat into the butter. Stir in the salt and cool slightly to blood temperature.

≈ Pour this egg and butter mixture over the floured yeast in the bowl. Stir with a wooden spoon and beat until the dough is thoroughly mixed.

≈ Knead the dough, by stretching and pulling with your hands until it is dry and smooth. If the dough is too soft, add a little more flour.

≈ Shape into a ball, place in the bowl and dust lightly with flour. Cover the bowl with a dish cloth. Leave to rise in a warm place for 20 minutes. The dough should at least double in volume.

≈ Knead through again and leave to rise for a further 20 minutes, covered. It is now ready for use.

≈ Grease and line a paella pan (dish for 2) with half the dough. Add the filling; remember the pie will rise to fill the pan.

≈ Cover with the slices of tomato and a little salt.

≈ Roll out the remaining dough, sealing the edges well. Glaze with the egg yolk and decorate as desired. Most Spanish cooks stick to a very simple pattern of thin crisscrossed strips.

≈ Leave to stand for 10 minutes before baking.

≈ Bake in a moderate to hot oven (200°C/400°F/gas 6) for 30 minutes. Leave to cool and slice.

FRIED SQUID

TO CLEAN THE SQUID

≈ Cut off the legs just below the eyes and keep to one side. Squeeze the top of the legs and the beak will pop out; discard it.

≈ Empty the body sac over the sink, by thrusting the fingers under the plastic-like backbone.

≈ Pull out the backbone and discard it.

≈ Pull the guts carefully, so that they come out in one piece, and discard. Rinse the inside of the sac.

≈ Remove the fins firmly from where they join the body. The purple membranous skin will then easily peel off.

≈ Rinse well and slice the body across into 1.25-cm/ ½-in thick rings. Combine with the legs and rinse again.

≈ Place in a pot of water on the stove, with enough water in to cover the squid. When boiling, add the squid. Bring back to the boil.

≈ Remove and cool immediately under cold water.

≈ The calamares (squid) are now ready for further use.

INGREDIENTS

3 eggs
1 kg/2lb squid, cleaned
salt and pepper
flour · 3 lemons

PREPARATION

≈ Mix the eggs well over the squid, using your hands. Season.

≈ Slowly add enough flour, mixing thoroughly to a thick paste.

≈ Heat the deep-fryer to 185°/365°F and carefully lower the squid piece by piece into the oil.

≈ Shake and fry to a golden colour.

≈ Remove, drain, sprinkle with salt and serve with plenty of lemon wedges.

NOTE: If your deep-fryer is too small to cook this all at once, cook in 2 or 3 batches, keeping the cooked squid warm until it is all ready.

Vegetables

······················

44
GAZPACHO

TOMATO SALAD WITH
MEDITERRANEAN VINAIGRETTE

45
STUFFED TOMATOES

46
GARLIC SOUP

47
GARLIC BREAD

48
GARLIC MUSHROOMS

49
CORN ON THE COB WITH GARLIC
BUTTER

PATATAS BRAVAS I

50
PATATAS BRAVAS II

51
ANCHOVY POTATO SALAD

52
CHEESE AND POTATO CROQUETTES

53
ASPARAGUS AND LETTUCE TARTS

54
PICKLED CUCUMBER WITH CHILLI

55
MINT AND CHILLI CUCUMBER

56
STEWED GIANT OLIVES

57
GREEN BEANS TAPA

60
REFRIED KIDNEY BEANS

61
ARTICHOKE HEARTS WITH TOMATO
AND LEMON

62
STUFFED COURGETTES (ZUCCHINI)

63
COURGETTES (ZUCCHINI) WITH DILL

64
STUFFED CABBAGE LEAVES

65
THREE PEPPERS IN TOMATO
AND GARLIC

66
STUFFED GREEN PEPPERS WITH
CHILLI MINCE

67
STUFFED GREEN PEPPERS WITH HAKE
AND CHEESE

68
AUBERGINE (EGGPLANT) WITH
CHEESE AND PRAWNS (SHRIMPS)

GAZPACHO

INGREDIENTS

1 *cucumber*
1 *green pepper, deseeded*
one 225g/8oz can of plum tomatoes
1 *medium onion*
1 *tsp garlic, crushed*
15ml/1 *tbsp lemon juice*
salt and black pepper

PREPARATION

≈ Blend all the ingredients in a food processor, season well and chill.

If you prefer a more liquid soup, add tomato juice and stir well.

TOMATO SALAD WITH MEDITERRANEAN VINAIGRETTE

This is lovely in summer with cheese and cold beer, or with anchovy fillets layered between the tomato and onion.

INGREDIENTS

3 *beef (large) tomatoes*
½ *onion, finley sliced*
a few black olives
1¼ *cups/¼l/½pt Mediterranean Vinaigrette (see Basic Recipes)*

PREPARATION

≈ Slice the tomatoes horizontally. Arrange either in a large bowl with onion in between layers, or on a large plate. Sprinkle with black olives.

≈ Dredge the toamtoes with the dressing and serve.

If keeping to serve later, add the dressing 20 minutes before required.

STUFFED TOMATOES

*You can use small tomatoes or large beef tomatoes for this recipe,
which is very simple and a colourful addition to any table.*

INGREDIENTS

8 *English (small) tomatoes, or 3 beef (large) tomatoes*

4 *hard-boiled eggs, cooled and peeled*

90ml/6tbsp *garlic mayonnaise (see Basic Recipes)*

salt and black pepper

1 tbsp *parsley, chopped*

1 tbsp *white breadcrumbs for the beef (large) tomatoes*

PREPARATION

≈ Skin the tomatoes, first by cutting out the core with a sharp knife and making a '+' incision on the other end of the tomato. Then place in a pan of boiling water for 10 seconds, remove and plunge into a bowl of iced or very cold water (this latter step is to stop the tomatoes from cooking and going mushy).

≈ Slice the tops off the tomatoes, and just enough of their bases to remove the rounded ends so that the tomatoes will sit squarely on the plate. Keep the tops if using small tomatoes, but not for the large tomatoes.

≈ Remove the seeds and inside, either with a tea-spoon or small, sharp knife.

≈ Mash the eggs with the mayonnaise, salt, pepper and parsley.

≈ Fill the tomatoes, firmly pressing the filling down. With small tomatoes, replace the lids at a jaunty angle. If keeping to serve later, brush them with olive oil and black pepper to prevent from drying out. Cover with plastic film and keep.

≈ For large tomatoes, the filling must be very firm, so it can be sliced. If you make your own mayonnaise, thicken it by using more egg yolks. If you use shop-bought mayonnaise, add enough white breadcrumbs until the mixture is the consistency of mashed pota-toes. Season well, to taste. Fill the tomatoes, pressing down firmly until level. Refrigerate for 1 hour, then slice with a sharp carving knife into rings. Sprinkle with chopped parsley.

GARLIC SOUP

INGREDIENTS

5 cups/1 ½pt chicken stock (*see Basic Recipes*)

3tsp garlic, crushed

3 level tsp paprika

3 level tsp cumin

salt and pepper

2 pieces of bread, toasted

oil

6 eggs (optional)

PREPARATION

≈ Pour chicken stock into a pan, add the garlic, paprika and cumin, and bring to the boil. Season.

≈ Break the toast into cubes and put into hot soup bowls.

≈ Place a pan on the heat, lightly oil and fry the eggs until the white forms. Tip out 1 egg into each soup bowl and pour over the boiling soup.

GARLIC BREAD

INGREDIENTS

1 large crusy loaf, or 6 small pitta breads

200g/½lb butter, softened to room temperature

2tsp garlic, peeled by placing on a tray in a hot oven for 10 minutes (the garlic will pop out of its skin)

1 tbsp parsley, chopped

salt and black pepper

PREPARATION

≈ Crush the peeled garlic cloves in a crusher, food processor or by the old-fashioned method of crushing under the blade of a large knife, with salt.

≈ Blend the crushed garlic into the butter. Add the chopped parsley and seasoning.

≈ Place the bread in a hot (230°C/450°F/gas 7) oven for 15 minutes. If using pitta breads, sprinkle with a little water before placing in the oven to give a softer bread.

≈ Slice the loaf, smother with the butter and serve.

There are several savoury alternatives to this recipe:

≈ Add 1 dessertspoon of tomato paste to the butter, smother slices of bread with the pink butter and toast.

≈ Use 150g/6oz butter and ½ cup/100g/4oz grated cheese, in place of the 200g/½lb butter. Mix together with the flavourings. Heat the bread, slice, smother with the cheesy butter and place back in the oven to melt the cheese. Season and serve.

47

GARLIC MUSHROOMS

INGREDIENTS

75g/3oz butter

750g/1½lb mushrooms, button or cap

a few drops of lemon juice

salt and black pepper

3tsp garlic, crushed

1tbsp coriander or parsley, chopped

PREPARATION

≈ Heat the butter in a large pan.

≈ Add the mushrooms and sweat gently, covered, for 5 minutes, shaking occasionally.

≈ Add the lemon juice, salt and pepper.

≈ Increase the heat, tossing the mushrooms well.

≈ Add the garlic, toss and cook for 2 minutes.

≈ Add the coriander or parsley and cook for 1 minute. Remove from the heat and serve.

CORN ON THE COB WITH GARLIC BUTTER

PREPARATION

≈ Remove the outher green leaves from the fresh corn. Place in boiling salted water with a drop of olive oil.

≈ Simmer for 20 minutes, or until the corn is cooked and tender.

≈ Remove from the heat and drain.

≈ Smother liberally with garlic butter (see recipe for Garlic Bread).

≈ Sprinkle with salt and freshly ground black pepper.

PATATAS BRAVAS I

INGREDIENTS

60ml / 4tbsp olive oil
8 medium-sized potatoes (peel and cut up if using old potatoes)
2 onions, chopped
15ml / 1tbsp chilli oil (see Basic Recipes)
8 slices good bacon, chopped
1 tsp garlic
salt and pepper

PREPARATION

≈ Heat the oil, add the potatoes; fry until cooked, stirring. Remove to a warm plate.

≈ Add the onions and chilli oil, and fry until soft. Add the bacon and toss until cooked, about 3–4 minutes. Add the garlic in the last 2 minutes so it does not burn. Season accordingly. Pour over the potatoes and serve.

PATATAS BRAVAS II

*These have a slightly sweet hot sauce
poured over them.*

INGREDIENTS

1 onion, chopped
30ml/2tbsp olive oil
1 bay leaf
2 red chilllies
2tsp garlic
1tbsp tomato paste
½tbsp sugar (up to 1tbsp, if the sauce is too tart for your liking)
1tbsp soy sauce
1 450g/1lb can plum tomatoes, chopped
1 glass of white wine
salt and black pepper
8 medium potatoes

PREPARATION FOR THE SAUCE

≈ Sweat the onions in the oil with the bay leaf.

≈ When soft, add the chillies, garlic, tomato paste, sugar and soy sauce. Sweat for a further 5 minutes on a low heat.

≈ Add the chopped tomatoes and white wine. Stir and bring to the boil. Simmer for 10 minutes. Taste and season.

This sauce should be slightly sweet; the flavour of the tomatoes should not dominate it.

PREPARATION FOR THE POTATOES

≈ Cut the potatoes like small roast potatoes.

≈ Grease a baking tray. Seaon the potatoes well and brush with melted butter.

≈ Roast in a hot oven, 230°C/450°F/gas 8, until golden.

≈ Pour the tomato sauce over the potatoes and serve.

ANCHOVY POTATO SALAD

INGREDIENTS

½kg/1lb potatoes, washed, peeled and cut into even shapes

1 tbsp puréed anchovies or anchovy essence

1¼ cups/60ml/½pt mayonnaise (see Basic Recipes)

2tsp parsley, chopped

½tsp freshly ground black pepper

PREPARATION

≈ Place the potatoes in a pot of water with salt, bring to the boil and simmer gently for approximately 10 minutes, or until just firm.

≈ Drain and cool under the cold tap.

≈ Blend the anchovy paste into the mayonnaise with the parsley and black pepper; taste. If you want a stronger anchovy paste, add more anchovy essence.

≈ Carefully stir in the potatoes. Serve.

CHEESE AND POTATO CROQUETTES

INGREDIENTS

1kg/2lb potatoes
2 egg yolks
50g/2oz butter
salt and pepper
pinch of nutmeg
dash of sherry
½ cup/100g/4oz grated Parmesan cheese
pinch of mustard
2tbsp parsley, chopped
seasoned flour
eggwash (egg beaten with a little milk)
breadcrumbs

PREPARATION

≈ Wash and peel the potatoes, and cut to an even size. Cook in salted water until soft; then drain.

≈ Put a lid on the pan of the potatoes and place over a low heat to dry out, stirring occasionally to prevent burning.

≈ Place the potatoes in a food processor with the yolks, butter and seasoning.

≈ Mix in the nutmeg, sherry, Parmesan cheese, mustard and parsley. The potatoes should be like a very firm mash. Overmixing will make them gluey, in which case some flour will have to be worked in by hand.

≈ Check that the mix is seasoned well and mould into cylinder shapes, 13×5cm (5×2in).

≈ Roll in seasoned flour; dip in eggwash and coat with breadcrumbs.

≈ Deep-fry in hot fat, 185°C/365°F. When golden, drain well and serve.

NOTE: If you want to keep the croquettes for cooking later, or the next day, place them carefully on a tray, cover with plastic film and refrigerate.

ASPARAGUS AND LETTUCE TARTS

Asparagus is a great favourite in Spain, but due to its price in other parts of the world, it is a good idea to stretch it out with lettuce — preferably iceberg, but any round lettuce will do.
If using fresh asparagus, keep back some of the tips for garnishing.

INGREDIENTS

½kg/1lb asparagus, fresh, or a 400g/1lb can of asparagus spears
juice of 1 lemon
1 medium-sized onion, finely chopped
50g/2oz butter
½ lettuce
1 tsp oiled garlic, crushed
salt and freshly ground pepper
30ml/2tbsp dry white wine
1¼ cups/¼al/½pt single (light) cream
4 eggs and 1 extra egg yolk
½ cup/100g/4oz cheese, preferably manchego
200g/½lb shortcrust patsry (see Basic Recipes)
1 20-cm/8-in flan ring, or 10 tartlet moulds

PREPARATION

≈ If using fresh asparagus, discard the stringy white root part of the asparagus and chop the rest into 1.25-cm (½-in) pieces. Keep the tips separate.

≈ Place the chopped asparagus in a pot of boiling salted water with the lemon juice added; keep back the tips.

≈ Simmer 8–10 minutes until just soft, adding the tips after 5 minutes.

≈ Remove from the heat, place a sieve over the pot and run cold water through it in the sink. The sieve will save the asparagus tips from breaking up.

≈ If using canned asparagus, drain well, and check that it is evenly chopped.

≈ Sweat the onion in the butter, that is, cook it gently covered until it is soft.

≈ Add the finely chopped lettuce to the onion and stir.

≈ Add the garlic and season.

≈ Add the white wine, stir and cook until the lettuce softens. If you need more liquid, add a little water. Cover and simmer for 5 minutes.

≈ Remove from the heat and allow to cool.

≈ Mix the asparagus with the onion and lettuce.

≈ Grease and flour 10 tartlet moulds, or 1 20-cm (8-in) flan ring, and rest in a cool place.

≈ Bake blind: cover the pastry with tin foil, fill the case with baking beans or rice, and cook in a hot oven (230°C/450°F/gas 7) for 5–8 minutes. Remove the foil and beans.

≈ Mix the cream with the eggs, and some salt and black pepper. Whisk well to break the egg white. Whisk in the grated cheese.

≈ Stir the lettuce and asparagus mix into the milk and egg mix, thoroughly blending the two so that the custard coats the vegetables.

≈ Spoon into the pastry moulds, placing the tips on top.

≈ Cook in a moderate oven (180°C/350°F/gas 4) for 10 minutes for tartlets or 15 minutes for flan-size.

The filling should be just firm to the touch and golden-brown when ready.

PICKLED CUCUMBER WITH CHILLI

This may sound horrible, but is actually quite delicious.
It also makes a great accompaniment for curries.

INGREDIENTS

2 cucumbers

salt

2 red chillies, or 15ml/1tbsp chilli oil (see Basic Recipes)

1 tsp garlic, crushed

freshly ground black pepper

white wine vinegar

sugar

PREPARATION

≈ Peel the cucumbers and slice finely.

≈ Spread on a tray and sprinkle with salt to remove the excess moisture. Leave for 2 hours.

≈ Wash the salt off the cucumbers, and drain.

≈ Chop the chillies, discarding the seeds.

≈ Mix the chillies with the cucumber and garlic, seasoning with freshly ground black pepper.

≈ Place in a jar, preferably a screw-top type or a jam jar with a covering.

≈ Cover with white wine vinegar and enough sugar to remove the acidity. Stir well and cover.

This may be eaten the next day — or even a year hence.

MINT AND CHILLI CUCUMBER

INGREDIENTS

1 *cucumber, grated, sprinkled with salt and placed in a sieve to remove excess moisture.*

1 *beef (large) tomato, peeled by placing in boiling water for 10 seconds and then plunged into cold water to remove skin*

½tsp *garlic, chopped*

bunch of mint, chopped

1 *small tub (container) of plain yoghurt*

1 *small tub (container) of soured cream*

1 tsp *cumin*

2 *red chillies, seeded and chopped*

salt and pepper

PREPARATION

≈ Wash the excess moisture off the cucumber and drain well, squeezing any moisture out.

≈ Chop the tomato into little squares; discard the seeds.

≈ Mix all the ingredients together in a bowl, season well and chill.

STEWED GIANT OLIVES

For 5 cups/ 1 ½pt olives

INGREDIENTS

1 jar large queen olives, cut around the pit without cutting through
1 onion, chopped
2tbsp garlic, crushed
1 bay leaf
30ml/ 2tbsp olive oil
30ml/ 2tbsp red wine vinegar

PREPARATION

≈ Put the ingredients in a pan. Cover with water, adding enough olive oil to put a slick on the top to protect the olives.

≈ Bring to the boil and simmer, covered, until soft, for 4–6 hours.

These will keep well, refrigerated for 2 weeks.

GREEN BEANS TAPA

INGREDIENTS

½kg/1lb green beans, topped and tailed

50g/2oz butter

¼ cup/60ml/2fl oz olive oil

½ medium onion, finely sliced

salt and pepper to taste

1¼ cups/250ml/½pt chicken stock (see Basic Recipes)

1 tbsp garlic, crushed

PREPARATION

≈ Place the beans in a pot of boiling salted water and cook for 6–8 minutes, until the beans are fairly firm but not raw. Drain well.

≈ Melt the butter in a pan, add the olive oil and heat.

≈ Add the onion, cook gently for 3–4 minutes.

≈ Add the beans, salt and pepper and toss. Add the chicken stock and the garlic.

≈ Cover and cook until tender, for about 10 minutes. Season well and serve.

Spectacular scenery, whether cultivated or apparently undiscovered and untouched by people, is as characteristic of southern Spain as its impressive architecture.

LEFT *Seville in a moment of midday peace*

CENTRE *Ronda is a town perched either side of a 1,000-ft gorge*

RIGHT AND OPPOSITE *a typical skyline and the parador (a hotel restored and run by the government) in Carmona*

REFRIED KIDNEY BEANS

This is a nice accompaniment to meat tapas.

INGREDIENTS

one 450g/1lb can kidney beans
1 red chilli
1 medium onion
2tsp garlic, crushed
1 tsp paprika
salt and black pepper
5 cups/1 ½pt water
6 slices good bacon, without the rind
¼ cup/50g/2oz butter

PREPARATION

≈ Place first 7 ingredients in a pan, bring to the boil and simmer for 40 minutes.

≈ Place one-quarter of the total in a food processor and purée. Remix the puréed beans with the whole beans.

≈ Chop the bacon.

≈ Place the bacon into boiling water for 10 minutes to remove the saltiness.

≈ Remove from the water and drain.

≈ Heat the butter in a frying pan and fry the bacon.

≈ Add the beans, little by little, and mash with the back of a spoon. Season well.

The beans should go into a purée, which is thick. Season, sprinkle with parsley and serve. The more often you refry the beans, the better they taste.

ARTICHOKE HEARTS
WITH TOMATO AND LEMON

INGREDIENTS

6 artichokes

1 tsp flour

2½ cups/ ½l/ 1 pt cold water

salt

juice of 1 lemon

TO PREPARE THE ARTICHOKES

≈ Cut off the stalks and pull out the underneath leaves.

≈ With a large knife, cut through the artichoke, leaving only about 2.5cm (1in) at the bottom of the vegetable.

≈ While holding the artichoke upside down, peel carefully with a small paring knife, removing all the leaf and any green part, and keeping the bottom as smooth as possible. If necessary, smooth with a peeler.

≈ Immediately rub with lemon and keep in lemon water.

≈ Use a teaspoon or your thumb to remove the furry choke in the centre. It should come out easily. If you have problems, don't worry: it will come out easily after cooking, though it will be a bit messy.

≈ Artichoke bottoms should always be cooked in a blanc to keep the colour.

TO COOK THE ARTICHOKES

≈ Mix the flour and water together, then add the salt and lemon juice.

≈ Strain through a sieve into a pan and bring to the boil, stirring constantly.

≈ Add the artichokes.

≈ Simmer gently until just tender, for about 20 minutes. Drain.

INGREDIENTS FOR THE SAUCE

75g/3oz butter

1 small onion, finely chopped

1 tsp garlic, crushed

4 slices good bacon, chopped, or smoked ham

one 225g/8oz can plum tomatoes or 2 beef (large) tomatoes, skinned, seeded and chopped

1oz parsley, chopped

salt and pepper

juice of 2 lemons

the 6 cooked artichoke bottoms

PREPARATION

≈ Melt the butter in a pan. Add the onion, garlic and bacon and cook gently for 5 minutes.

≈ Add the tomato and parsley. Season and bring to the boil.

≈ Add the lemon juice.

≈ Add the artichoke bottoms cut into 5 or 6 triangles, by cutting each one in half, then each half into 2 or 3.

≈ Heat gently, stirring. If the mix is too tart, add a pinch of sugar.

Serve with crusty bread and a tomato salad.

STUFFED COURGETTES (ZUCCHINI)

INGREDIENTS

6 small courgettes (zucchini)

½ medium onion, finely chopped

15ml/1 tbsp olive oil

200g/½lb lamb, minced (ground)

3 slices good bacon, finely chopped

salt and freshly ground black pepper

1 tsp tomato paste

½tsp sugar

1 tsp garlic, crushed

15ml/1 tbsp water

1 tomato, peeled and chopped

½ small tub (container) plain yoghurt

12 mint leaves, chopped

¼ cup/50g/2oz grated Parmesan cheese

1 tbsp parsley, chopped

PREPARATION

≈ Trim off the ends of the courgettes (zucchini) and place them in boiling salted water for 5 minutes. Cut in half lengthwise and, with a teaspoon, scoop out the seeds along the centre.

≈ Cook the onion in the oil gently until soft.

≈ Add the minced (ground) lamb, bacon, salt and pepper. Stir.

≈ Add the tomato paste, sugar, garlic and water.

≈ Cook until the meat is cooked, for about 15 minutes.

≈ Stir in the chopped tomato, yoghurt and chopped mint leaves.

≈ Spoon this mix into the hollowed-out courgettes (zucchini). Sprinkle with the Parmesan cheese and black pepper. Bake in a hot oven (200°C/400°F/gas 6) until the cheese melts. Sprinkle over with parsley and serve.

COURGETTES (ZUCCHINI) WITH DILL

INGREDIENTS

¼ cup/60ml/2fl oz olive oil

25g/1oz butter

1 onion, chopped

1tsp garlic, crushed

½kg/1lb courgettes (zucchini), topped, tailed and sliced in thickish rounds

½tsp black pepper

2tsp paprika

1 tbsp dill, chopped (not the stalks)

1 small tub (container) soured cream

salt to taste

PREPARATION

≈ Heat oil and butter in a large frying pan. Cook the onion and garlic gently until soft. Turn up the heat.

≈ Add the courgettes (zucchini), garlic and black pepper and toss.

≈ Cook for 5–10 minutes, stirring to cook both sides of the courgette (zucchini) slices.

≈ When browning, add the paprika, dill and soured cream. Season and serve.

If you would like to use this as a vegetable to accompany a meat dish, try grating the courgettes (zucchini) and adding 30ml/2tbsp double (heavy) cream.

STUFFED CABBAGE LEAVES

For this recipe, you may substitute large spinach or cos-lettuce leaves for the cabbage.

INGREDIENTS

1 *large green cabbage*
1 *tsp paprika*
salt and pepper
½*tbsp parsley, chopped*
½*kg/1lb lamb, minced (ground)*
50*g/2oz butter*
1 *onion, finely chopped*
1*tsp garlic, crushed*
1 *red chilli, seeded and chopped*
1*tsp tomato paste*
1 *glass of tomato juice*
1*tsp soy sauce*
1¼ *cups/250ml/½pt chicken stock (see Basic Recipes)*
½ *cup/100g/4oz mushrooms, finely chopped*
⅜ *cup/75g/3oz salted peanuts, crushed*

TO PREPARE THE CABBAGE

≈ Remove the dirty outer leaves from the cabbage. Carefully pick off the large whole leaves and cut out the thick part of the stalk.

≈ Put the leaves in a pot of boiling salted water to soften. Simmer for 5 minutes.

≈ Remove the leaves and plunge into cold water.

≈ When cold, carefully lay out the leaves on a clean dish cloth, and pat dry with another dish cloth placed on top. Arrange with the inside of the leaves facing towards you.

TO PREPARE THE FILLING

≈ In a large bowl work the paprika, salt, pepper and parsley into the minced (ground) lamb.

≈ Melt the butter in a pot. Add the onion and cook gently until softened.

≈ Add the lamb, garlic, chilli and tomato paste.

≈ Pour in the tomato juice, soy sauce and stock, and stir. Add the mushrooms and peanuts.

≈ Simmer for 30 minutes, stirring occasionally. Remove from the heat and cool. Check the seasoning. If the mixture is still runny, add a small amount of flour.

≈ When cold, spoon small amounts of the mixture into the centre of the cabbage leaves, folding the outside edges over and placing the folded side, base down, in an oiled baking dish.

NOTE: If your leaves are a bit ragged or small, use two leaves to wrap around the lamb mixture.

≈ When all the cabbage parcels are in the baking dish, pour in enough chicken stock to half-cover them. Cover the tray with tin foil. Pierce with a fork to allow the steam to escape and poach in the oven for 20 minutes, at 200°C/400°F/gas 6.

≈ Remove carefully with a large spoon and moisten with a little of the poaching liqueur.

THREE PEPPERS IN TOMATO AND GARLIC

*This is a summer tapa, and may be eaten hot or cold;
its flavour improves after one day.*

INGREDIENTS

¾ cup/150ml/6fl oz olive oil

2 yellow peppers, deseeded and cut into thin strips

2 red peppers, deseeded and cut into thin strips

2 green peppers, deseeded and cut into thin strips

1 tbsp parsley, chopped

2 tsp garlic, crushed

225g/8oz of fresh or canned tomatoes

salt and pepper

PREPARATION

≈ Heat the oil in a large frying pan and cook the peppers gently for 2–3 minutes, stirring frequently. Add the parsley and garlic and cook for another couple of minutes.

≈ Add the chopped tomatoes and their juice to the pan. Stir and season.

≈ Cover the pan and simmer gently for about 20 minutes, until the peppers are tender.

≈ The sauce should be quite thick — if necessary, remove the peppers and boil rapidly to reduce the liquid. Check the seasoning.

NOTE: If you like spicy food, substitute chilli oil for the olive oil (see Basic Recipes).

STUFFED GREEN PEPPERS
WITH CHILLI MINCE

INGREDIENTS

1 onion, finely chopped

¼ cup/60ml/2fl oz oil (or 50g/2oz butter)

3 large or 6 small green peppers

½kg/1lb minced (ground) beef or pork

2tsp garlic, crushed

6 red chillies, finely chopped

½tsp oregano

1 bay leaf

2½ cups/½l/1pt water

salt and pepper

2tsp tomato paste

1tsp basil, chopped

2 beef (large) tomatoes, peeled and chopped

one 225g/8oz can kidney beans

½ cup/100g/4oz grated manchego cheese

TO PREPARE THE FILLING

≈ Gently cook the onion in the oil or butter.

≈ Add the meat, garlic, chillies, oregano, bay leaf, water, salt, pepper, tomato paste and basil, and cook, stirring, until it reaches the boil.

≈ Lower heat and simmer for 45 minutes, stirring occasionally.

≈ Add the beans and tomato, season to taste and bring to the boil. Remove from heat.

TO PREPARE THE PEPPERS

≈ Remove the stalks. Plunge into boiling salted water and simmer for 5 minutes.

≈ Immediately cool in cold water and drain.

≈ If peppers are large, cut in half lengthwise, and remove seeds.
Fill with meat mixture.

≈ Sprinkle with cheese and bake at 200°C/400°F/gas 6, until the cheese melts.

≈ If the peppers are small, cut off the tops and keep them aside.

≈ Carefully remove the seeds and core.

≈ Trim base so that the pepper will sit squarely, without making a hole in it.

≈ Fill and sprinkle with cheese.

≈ Place on a baking tray with the top next to it to heat up. When cheese is melted, replace top and serve.

STUFFED GREEN PEPPERS
WITH HAKE AND CHEESE

INGREDIENTS

3 large or 6 small green peppers

½kg/1lb hake

salt and pepper

5 cups/1l/2pt milk

100g/4oz butter

½ cup/100g/4oz flour

pinch of nutmeg

1 cup/200g/8oz grated manchego cheese

TO PREPARE THE PEPPERS

≈ Put peppers in a pan of boiling salted water. Cover and simmer for 5 minutes or until softened.

≈ Drain and cool. Remove seeds and any pith. For small peppers, keep the top and trim the base so that they stand squarely. For large peppers, cut in half lengthwise.

TO PREPARE THE FILLING

≈ Skin and bone the fish, place in a roasting pan, season and pour over the milk. Cook in a hot oven (220°C/425°C/gas 7), until the fish flakes.

≈ Drain off the milk and keep. Place the fish to one side.

≈ Melt the butter in a pot. Stir in the flour and cook to a sandy texture, stirring frequently.

≈ Add the fishy milk a little at a time, beating to a paste with a wooden spoon.

≈ When all the milk is added, stir and simmer for 15 minutes to cook the flour.

≈ Add the nutmeg and cheese, and simmer until it melts.

≈ Stir in the flaked fish.

≈ Season, remove from heat and spoon into the peppers.

≈ Place on a baking sheet and place in a medium-hot oven (230°C/450°F/gas 8) for 10 minutes.

AUBERGINE (EGGPLANT) WITH CHEESE AND PRAWNS (SHRIMPS)

INGREDIENTS

1 large aubergine (eggplant)
salt
⅛ cup/50g/2oz flour
olive oil
1¼ cups/250ml/½pt thick cheese sauce (see below)

PREPARATION

≈ Prepare the aubergine (eggplant). This will need to be degorged: slice finely across into thin rounds, spread the slices in a large tray and sprinkle with salt. Leave for 20 minutes to remove excess moisture. Pat dry with a dish cloth or paper towel.

≈ Pass through flour, shaking off any excess.

≈ In a large frying pan, pour in enough olive oil to comfortably cover the base and heat.

≈ Place the floured aubergine (eggplant) rounds into the oil and fry on each side until golden.

≈ Remove and drain on paper towel or greaseproof paper. Arrange carefully and keep to one side.

FOR THE CHEESE SAUCE

(Note: This might be slightly thicker than the sauce you normally might use)

INGREDIENTS

50g/2oz butter
¼ cup/50g/2oz flour
1¼ cups/250ml/½pt milk, warmed
½ small onion
1 bay leaf
pinch of nutmeg
⅔ cup/75g/3oz grated manchego or Parmesan cheese
15ml/1 tbsp cream
1 egg yolk
salt and pepper

PREPARATION

≈ Melt the butter in a pan.

≈ Stir in the flour and cook gently to a paste.

≈ Add the warmed milk gradually, stirring all the time until smooth.

≈ Add the onion, bay leaf and nutmeg, and cook gently for 20 minutes to cook the flour.

≈ Strain through a sieve.

≈ Stir in the cheese and the cream

≈ Remove from heat and beat in the egg yolk. Season.

≈ Mix the prawns (shrimps) into the sauce.

≈ Arrange the aubergine (eggplant) slices on a baking tray.

≈ Spoon over the cheese and prawn (shrimp) sauce.

≈ Sprinkle with the grated Parmesan cheese and place in the oven at 200°C/400°F/gas 6, until golden-brown. Serve on small plates.

Egg and Cheese

....

70

GOAT'S CHEESE WITH TARRAGON
AND GARLIC MARINADE

71

CHILLI MANCHEGO

72

TORTILLA ESPAÑOLA

73

PAELLA CROQUETTES

74

EGG AND GARLIC FRIED BREAD

GOAT'S CHEESE WITH TARRAGON
AND GARLIC MARINADE

*Try to get genuine manchego goat's cheese, which is
firm and has a lovely mild, milky flavour. Don't
remove the rind; chop into even chunks and marinate.*

PREPARATION

≈ Cover the cheese with olive oil and:
15ml/1tbsp white wine vinegar per 2pt/1l oil
1 bunch of tarragon, with crushed stalks
1 bulb of garlic per qt/1l oil
Black peppercorns
≈ Leave for at least 4 days in a jar or porcelain pot
before eating.

CHILLI MANCHEGO

This is a spicy tapa — serve it with plenty of crusty bread,
a wedge of lime and ice-cold beer.

INGREDIENTS

6 red chillies, seeded and chopped

1 cup / 250ml / 8fl oz olive oil

salt and pepper

2 cups / 400g / 1lb manchego cheese

PREPARATION

≈ Blend the chillies with the olive oil, adding a good pinch each of salt and pepper.

≈ Cut the cheese into small, spikable cubes.

≈ Pour the oil over the cheese and marinate for at least 2 hours.

TORTILLA ESPAÑOLA

BASIC RECIPE FOR 1 TORTILLA

INGREDIENTS

3 potatoes (or an equal amount of potato to onion)
45ml/3tbsp olive oil
1 onion, finely chopped or sliced
salt and black pepper
3 eggs

PREPARATION

NOTE: When frying, if the mixture becomes a little too dry, add more oil.

≈ Wash the potatoes. (It is optional to peel them — Spaniards will never put unpeeled potato in a tortilla, but I find other people like to.) Slice very finely and place in a pot of cold salted water. Bring to the boil and cook for 5 minutes (parboil). If preferred, the potatoes for this dish can be sautéed.

≈ Place a frying pan on the heat. Pour in the oil and get it very hot.

≈ Add the onion very carefully, as the oil might spit. Toss.

≈ Add the potato slices. Shake the pan, and stir to prevent any sticking to the bottom. Season lightly with salt and pepper.

≈ In a bowl, beat the eggs and season well.

≈ Lower the heat slightly on the potatoes and onions and cook, tossing until golden-brown.

≈ Tip the potato and onion into the egg mix, and mix well.

≈ Replace the pan on the heat and when hot pour the mixture into it. It will seal immediately. Cook for 2 minutes, then turn the tortilla by one of 2 methods:

Either slip the tortilla into another hot pan brushed with oil by placing pan no. 2 over pan no. 1 and flipping it, or

Place a large plate over the tortilla and turn out onto the plate. Push the tortilla off the plate, back into the pan so that the uncooked side is now over the heat.

Many ingredients and flavouring may be used (or used up!) in tortillas, for instance, green peppers (sliced and added to the onions), mushrooms, cooked ham, cheese and so on.

PAELLA CROQUETTES

These make an ideal savoury finger-food.

INGREDIENTS

2 cups/400g/1lb short-grain rice

1 medium onion, roughly chopped

1 bay leaf

1 tsp garlic, crushed

1 tsp chicken bouillon (or 1 stock cube)

15ml/1 tbsp olive oil

2 tsp turmeric

3 times the quantity of water to rice (ideally, use good chicken stock, see Basic Recipes)

250g/10oz chorizo sausage and smoked ham, mixed, preferably in equal quantities (any spicy salamis or cooked meats may be used for this recipe)

seasoned flour

eggs, beaten with a little milk

breadcrumbs

PREPARATION

≈ Put the rice in a pot, add the onion, bay leaf, garlic, bouillon, olive oil and turmeric. Pour on the hot water.

≈ Put on the heat and bring to the boil. Simmer until soft and the rice has saturated the water, stirring occasionally.

≈ Remove from heat and leave to cool.

≈ Mince the meat in a mincer or food processor.

≈ Add the meat to the cold rice, mixing in well. The mixture should be slightly moist but easy to form into small balls. If your mix is too wet, add a little flour or breadcrumbs to it.

≈ Form the mix into balls. There should be an equal ratio of rice to meat in the balls.

≈ Roll the rice balls in the flour until lightly covered.

≈ Roll in the eggwash and then in the breadcrumbs. At this stage the croquettes may be refrigerated and kept until the next day.

≈ Deep-fry in hot oil, 185°C/365°F, until golden and crispy on the outside. These may be microwaved to reheat.

EGG AND GARLIC FRIED BREAD

INGREDIENTS

3 eggs, beaten

a few drops of warm water

2tsp garlic, crushed

salt and pepper

6 slices of bread

45ml/3tbsp olive oil

PREPARATION

≈ Beat the eggs in a bowl with a few drops of warm water.

≈ Add the crushed garlic and seasoning to the egg and mix well.

≈ Heat a frying pan, pour in the oil and heat.

≈ Dip the bread in the egg so that both sides are covered.

≈ Place each piece of bread in the frying pan.

≈ Fry until each side is golden brown.

The oil must be hot for this recipe to seal the egg immediately (watch for a wavy look on the pan bottom). Also, the bread must be turned quickly to prevent the garlic from burning.

Chicken and Quail

····················

76

CHICKEN IN GARLIC SAUCE

77

CHICKEN IN BATTER WITH HONEY
AND MUSTARD

78

STUFFED CHICKEN BREASTS

79

CHICKEN EMPANADA

BACON AND CHICKEN WITH MUSSELS

80

CHICKEN LIVERS WITH SHERRY
VINEGAR

82

STUFFED QUAILS

CHICKEN IN GARLIC SAUCE

This is quick dish, and care should be taken not to overcook the chicken pieces.

INGREDIENTS

1kg/2lb chicken wings, or 3 breasts

enough seasoned flour to coat the chicken pieces

¼ cup/60ml/2fl oz olive oil

25g/1oz butter

½ glass of white wine

3tsp garlic, crushed

1tbsp parsley, chopped

20ml/⅙ gill of sherry

20ml/⅙ gill of brandy

salt and pepper

PREPARATION

≈ Cut the chicken into small chunks. Toss it in seasoned flour.

≈ Put the oil and butter in a pan and get them hot.

≈ Put the chicken pieces in the pan, stirring quickly to seal all sides.

≈ Add the wine, garlic and parsley.

≈ Reduce the wine by half and add the chicken stock. Stir.

≈ At this stage, the smaller pieces of chicken may be cooked; if so, remove them and put them aside.

≈ Add the sherry and brandy.

≈ Season and serve.

CHICKEN IN BATTER WITH HONEY AND MUSTARD

INGREDIENTS

3 chicken breasts, cut into 2.54-cm/1-in cubes

salt and pepper

2 eggs

flour to coat

60ml/4tbsp olive oil

½ cup/120ml/4fl oz runny honey

5ml/1tsp French mustard

5ml/1tsp soy sauce

PREPARATION

≈ Place the chicken pieces in a bowl. Season.

≈ Break the eggs over the chicken pieces and mix in thoroughly, using your hands.

≈ Add enough flour to make a thick coating over the chicken. The egg and flour mixture should be of a consistency where it only just does not drip.

≈ Heat the oil in a pan and fry the chicken until golden, turning frequently, for about 15 minutes.

≈ Remove from the heat, sprinkle with salt and pepper.

≈ Blend the honey with the mustard and soy sauce.

≈ Pour the honey mixture over the chicken and serve immediately.

STUFFED CHICKEN BREASTS

These may be served hot or cold, sliced.

INGREDIENTS

3 *large chicken breasts, with wing bone still attached*
½*cup/100g/4oz green seedless grapes*
¼ *cup/50g/2oz ground almonds*
1 *cup/200g/8oz cream cheese, softened to room temperature*
1 *egg, beaten*
salt and freshly ground black pepper
1¼ *cups/250ml/½pt chicken stock (see Basic Recipes), or poaching liqueur (see below)*

PREPARATION

≈ Prepare the stuffing:
Peel the grapes, by placing in boiling water for 10 seconds and immediately plunging into cold water. The skins will come off easily.
Roughly chop the grapes and mix well with the almonds, cream cheese and beaten egg.
Refrigerate for 30 minutes.

INGREDIENTS FOR POACHING LIQUEUR

25g/1oz *butter*
¼ *medium onion*
1¼ *cup/250ml/½pt chicken stock (see Basic Recipes)*
1 *bay leaf*
1 *glass of white wine*
6 *peppercorns*

TO PREPARE POACHING LIQUEUR

≈ Melt the butter in a small roasting tray, add the onion and all the other ingredients. Bring to the boil.
≈ Prepare the chicken breasts:
Remove the thin strip of fillet from the breast.
Take hold of the wine bone in the left hand and with a small, sharp knife, make 2 incisions lengthwise, by sliding the blade out to the edges but without cutting right through the flesh.
Lightly flatten the fillets.
Stuff the pockets of the chicken breast, comfortably — not to bursting capacity.
Replace the fillet along the top of the stuffing to seal it in and close the cut flaps of the chicken breast over it, thus forming a sealed envelope.

NOTE: If, when making the pocket in the chicken, you cut right through and have a hole, brush over with egg white prior to cooking or your stuffing will burst out.

≈ Season the chicken and poach lightly in chicken stock of poaching liqueur for approximately 20 minutes at 220°C/425°F/gas 7, or until firm to the touch.

If serving hot, leave to sit for a couple of minutes and slice across with a sharp knife. Strain the liquid and place back on the heat to reduce. Coat the chicken with the liquid.

If serving cold, remove from poaching liqueur and cool. Refrigerate for a couple of hours and slice with a sharp knife.

These chicken pieces are delicious served with garlic toast:
≈ Take 6 thick slices of bread and stamp out rings with a large round pastry cutter.
≈ Brush a baking tray (cookie sheet) with olive oil.
≈ Prepare some garlic butter (see Basic Recipes).
≈ Smother the rounds of bread with garlic butter and bake in a hot oven (230°C/450°F/gas 8) for 10 minutes until crisp around the edges.

Place a slice of chicken on the garlic toast, arrange on a large plate and pass around.

CHICKEN EMPANADA

Note: If you wish to make individual empanadas, cut out 15-cm/6-in rounds of pastry. Place the filling in one half and cover with the remaining dough, sealing well.

INGREDIENTS

2¼ cups/450g/18oz yeast dough, as for recipe for Squid Espanada

¼ cup/50g/2oz butter

INGREDIENTS FOR THE FILLING

60ml/4tbsp olive oil

1 onion, chopped

200g/½lb streaky bacon, chopped

3tsp garlic, crushed

1 green pepper, seeded and sliced

2 chillies, seeded and chopped

1tsp paprika

¾ cup/150g/6oz button mushrooms, sliced

⅔ cup/75g/3oz raisins (optional)

10g/2tsp parsley, chopped

10ml/2tsp soy sauce

1 glass of dry white wine

1¼ cups/250ml/½pt chicken stock (see Basic Recipe)

25g/1oz butter

1kg/2lb chicken meat, boned and cubed

BACON AND CHICKEN WITH MUSSELS

INGREDIENTS

¼ cup/60ml/2fl oz olive oil

1 onion, chopped

6 slices of good bacon, cut into strips

3 chicken breasts, cubed and tossed in seasoned flour

2 cups/400g/1lb mushrooms, finely sliced

2tsp garlic, crushed

salt and freshly ground black pepper

1 glass of dry white wine

2½ cups/½l/1pt fish or chicken stock (see Basic Recipes)

1kg/2lb mussels, cleaned and debearded

30g/2tbsp parsley, chopped

PREPARATION

≈ Heat the oil. Gently cook the onion and bacon in it.
≈ Add the garlic, green pepper, chillies, paprika, sliced mushrooms, and raisins, if used. Stir and add the parsley and soy sauce.
≈ Pour on the wine and stock, stir, and simmer for 20 minutes.
≈ In a separate pan, melt the butter and add the chicken cubes. Toss until browned all over and add to the vegetables. Stir and simmer for 5 minutes.
≈ Remove from heat.
≈ Fill empanada as in recipe for Squid Empanada and cook as before.

PREPARATION

≈ Heat the oil in a pan. Add the onion and cook gently.
≈ Turn up the heat, add the bacon and stir.
≈ Add the chicken pieces and stir again to seal the meat all over.
≈ Take the wine mushrooms and garlic, reduce by one-half separately in a pot, then add to the chicken.
≈ Add the chicken or fish stock and bring to the boil.
≈ Add the mussels. Cover the pan with a lid and shake.
≈ Cook until the mussels open. Season well, spoon into hot bowls and garnish with parsley.

CHICKEN LIVERS WITH SHERRY VINEGAR

INGREDIENTS

1 tsp paprika
1 tsp garlic
½tsp salt
½tsp black pepper
½kg/1lb chicken livers, trimmed (to remove any gristle and the green bile sacs) and washed
50g/2oz butter, melted
½ onion, finely chopped
¼ cup/60ml/2fl oz sherry vinegar
1 tsp sugar
1¼ cups/250ml/½pt chicken stock (see Basic Recipes)
50g/2oz unsalted butter

PREPARATION

≈ Mix the paprika, garlic, salt and pepper together in a bowl. Toss the livers in, mixing the seasoning well over them.

≈ Heat a large frying pan, add the melted butter and get it hot.

≈ Turn the livers into the pan, stirring immediately over high heat. Keep tossing to seal the livers and brown all over.

≈ Remove livers to a warmed bowl.

≈ Add the onion to the pan and soften over a lower heat.

≈ Turn up the heat again, add the vinegar and sugar. Cook until the vinegar is almost dry.

≈ Add the stock, stir and reduce to half the quantity.

≈ Take the remaining 50g/2oz butter, break into small pieces and shake into the pan until it is all absorbed.

≈ Check the seasoning and pour over the livers, either in one large bowl or several smaller, individual ones.

STUFFED QUAILS

INGREDIENTS

---

6 *quails*

INGREDIENTS FOR THE FILLING

---

1 *chicken breast*

---

1 *egg white*

---

salt and pepper

⅝ *cup/125ml/¼pt double (heavy) cream*

¼ *cup/50g/2oz raisins*

¼ *cup/50g/2oz whole almonds, blanched and roughly chopped*

---

pinch of nutmeg

INGREDIENTS FOR THE POACHING LIQUID

3¾ *cups/¾l/1½pt stock*

---

2 *parsley stalks*

---

1 *bay leaf*

---

1 *shot of port*

50g/2oz *unsalted butter*

PREPARATION

≈ Bone the quails, using a small, very sharp knife. Your butcher might already do this for you. If not:
Place the quail on its breast and cut along the backbone from neck to tail.
Use the blade of the knife to guide you under the skin and around the carcass of the bird until you reach the breastbone.
Because of the size of the quail, it is difficult to guide you in theory around the carcass. The most important point to remember is not to cut through the skin. If necessary, crush the carcass around the wing area and remove the bones in pieces.
Once you have done one and have a whole quail before you splayed out on the table, the leg bones kept in, the picture becomes much clearer.
Use the bones for stock.

≈ Season the quail meat and keep in the refrigerator while you make the stuffing.

TO PREPARE THE FILLING

≈ Trim any sinews and fat from the chicken breast.
≈ Roughly chop and place the chicken in a food processor with the egg whites. Whizz.
NOTE: Everything used must now be thoroughly chilled and any mixing must be done over ice.

≈ Season the mix.
≈ Over a bowl of ice, gradually beat in the double (heavy) cream with a wooden spoon.
≈ Fold in the raisins, nutmeg and almonds.
≈ Season well, as the cream and egg white will cause the mixture to become bland during cooking.
≈ Spread out the quail skins.
≈ Divide the stuffing into six and lay down the centre of the quails, moulding into a neat roll.
≈ Neatly fold the flaps of skin over the stuffing, tucking in any loose ends. The quail should resemble a fat sausage, not a pear or a tube of toothpaste!
≈ Take a needle and thread (use a colour that will show up well when the quail is cooked) and, with half a dozen neat stitches, sew the quail together.

(NOTE: From experience, coloured dental floss is perfect for this trussing.)

≈ To cook the quail:
Heat 50g/2oz butter in a pan.
Seal the quails in the hot fat and place in a roasting pan.
Pour in the poaching liquid, bring to the boil and season. Poach in a hot oven, at 230°C/450°F/gas 8, for 30 minutes, or until firm to the touch.
≈ Remove the quails from the liquid, and reduce it by half over the heat. Shake in the unsalted butter, little piece by little piece. Add the port, season. Remove from the heat.
≈ Once out of the oven, leave the quails to rest for a couple of minutes. Remove the thread or dental floss, which should be quite an easy task if you sewed it up simply. With a sharp knife, slice the quail into 3 or 4 pieces, put on a plate and pour the sauce over.

This may be eaten cold; in which case, don't worry about the sauce.

Meat

······················

84
JAMÓN SERRANO

JAMÓN SERRANO WITH TOMATO
AND GARLIC TOAST

87
BLOOD SAUSAGE WITH TOMATO
AND GARLIC

88
MEATBALLS WITH GARLIC AND
TOMATO

89
MARINATED LAMB CUTLETS

LAMB WITH APRICOT SAUCE

90
KIDNEYS IN SHERRY SAUCE

91
VEAL SWEETBREADS IN GARLIC AND
OLIVE OIL

92
CHUNKED PORK IN ORANGE SAUCE

93
CALDO GALLEGO SOUP

BAKED CHORIZO SAUSAGE

JAMÓN SERRANO

Jamón serrano is a smoked ham from Spain. It is usually served thinly sliced and is also delicious with melon (as is Italian prosciutto).

INGREDIENTS

300g/¾lb jamón serrano, prosciutto or Westphalian ham, finely sliced and rolled

2½ cups/1pt stuffed olives

2 lemons, cut into wedges

PREPARATION

≈ Spike cocktail sticks with a roll of ham and an olive, alternately, and serve with lemon wedges.

JAMÓN SERRANO WITH TOMATO AND GARLIC TOAST

INGREDIENTS

6 slices of garlic bread

2 beef (large) tomatoes, sliced and dredged with Mediterranean Vinaigrette (see Basic Recipes)

200g/½lb jamón serrano, prosciutto or Westphalian ham, finely sliced

1 red onion, sliced finely

½ cup/100g/4oz stuffed olives, chopped

PREPARATION

≈ Prepare the garlic bread and bake in a hot oven until crisp around the edges.

≈ On the toast place a slice of tomato, a slice of ham and top with sliced onion and chopped olives.

BLOOD SAUSAGE WITH TOMATO AND GARLIC

INGREDIENTS

⅛ cup/30ml/1fl oz olive oil

2 black puddings (blood sausage), sliced thinly

50g/2oz butter

1 onion, chopped

one 225g/8oz can plum tomatoes, chopped

2tsp garlic, crushed

1oz parsley, chopped

salt and black pepper

PREPARATION

≈ Heat the oil in a large pan.

≈ Add the blood sausage and cook quickly, tossing to prevent burning.

≈ When cooked on each side, tip the slices onto a tray and keep warm in the oven.

≈ Melt the butter in the pan.

≈ Add the chopped onion and sweat gently, for about 5 minutes.

≈ Add the tomatoes, garlic, parsley, salt and pepper.

≈ Cook for 5 minutes; season.

Pour the sauce over the black puddings and serve garnished with parsley.

MEATBALLS WITH GARLIC AND TOMATO

These may be prepared ahead of time and reheated.

INGREDIENTS

1kg/2lb lamb, minced (ground)

¼ cup/50g/2oz breadcrumbs

salt and black pepper

2tsp garlic, crushed

½tsp nutmeg

2 eggs

¼ cup/50g/2oz seasoned flour

¼ cup/60ml/2fl oz olive oil

1 large onion, chopped

1 green pepper, cut into strips

one 225g/8oz can chopped plum tomatoes, or two beef (large) tomatoes, skinned and roughly chopped

1 tbsp tomato paste

1 glass of dry red wine

⅝ cup/375ml/¾pt chicken stock (see Basic Recipes)

1 tbsp parsley, chopped

PREPARATION

≈ In a large bowl, mix the lamb with the breadcrumbs and season well. Add 1tsp of the crushed garlic, the nutmeg and the eggs.

≈ Form into small meatballs, then roll in the flour.

≈ Heat the oil in a large pot, and cook the onion and green pepper until tender.

≈ Add the meatballs and fry until browned on all sides, stirring well.

≈ Add the remaining garlic, the tomatoes, tomato paste, wine and stock. Cover and simmer for 40 minutes.

≈ Season, stir in the parsley and serve. Add a little sugar if the sauce is too sharp.

MARINATED LAMB CUTLETS

This is a very simple and popular tapa.

INGREDIENTS

6 lamb cutlets, trimmed of excess fat

INGREDIENTS FOR THE MARINADE

2tsp paprika

1tsp cumin

1tsp turmeric

1 chopped red chilli

½ bunch of chopped mint

60ml/4tbsp olive oil

TO PREPARE THE MARINADE

≈ Mix all the ingredients for the marinade together and brush liberally all over the cutlets.

≈ Leave in the refrigerator for at least 1 hour.

≈ To cook, either grill under a hot grill or bake in the oven for 10 minutes, or until tender.

Although these cutlets don't really need a sauce, I like to use a dip of *crème fraiche* with a purée of dried apricot, made with:
200g/8oz tub (container) of *crème fraiche*
50g/2oz dried apricots, chopped in a food processor
freshly ground black pepper

LAMB WITH APRICOT SAUCE

INGREDIENTS

¾kg/1½lb lamb fillet, cut into 2.54-cm/1-in cubes, seasoned

PREPARATION

≈ The lamb may be spiked onto skewers and grilled; or tossed in a pan with hot oil or melted butter, and cooked until tender, for about 5 minute.

INGREDIENTS FOR THE SAUCE

¼ cup/60ml/2fl oz vegetable oil

50g/2oz butter

1tsp garlic, crushed

150g/6oz canned apricots, puréed

75g/3oz peanut butter

lemon juice to taste, about 1 lemon's worth

salt and black pepper

TO PREPARE THE SAUCE

≈ Melt the oil and butter together. Add the garlic.

≈ Whisk in the puréed apricots and the peanut butter.

≈ Do now allow the peanut butter to become too hot; ideally, remove from the pan when half-dissolved.

≈ Add the lemon juice and season to taste.

≈ Pour over the lamb pieces.

KIDNEYS IN SHERRY SAUCE

INGREDIENTS

¾kg/1½lb lamb or veal kidneys

¾ cup/180ml/6fl oz olive oil

2tsp garlic, crushed

1tsp paprika

2 onions, chopped

1 glass of sherry

1¼ cups/250ml/½pt chicken stock (see Basic Recipes)

salt and pepper

4tsp parsley, chopped

3 slices of bread

PREPARATION

≈ Clean the kidneys, removing any fat and the hard core. Slice thinly with a sharp knife.

≈ Bring a pot of water to the boil and plunge the kidneys in to remove the bitterness.

≈ Heat the oil and fry half the kidneys, with 1tsp of the garlic and ½tsp of the paprika

≈ Cook quickly, stirring so the garlic does not burn.

≈ When cooked, blend in a food processor. Keep to one side.

≈ In the same pan cook the onions until soft.

≈ Place the remaining kidneys in the pan with the other 1tsp of the garlic and ½tsp of paprika, as well as with the sherry and stock. Bring to the boil.

≈ Lower the heat, add the puréed kidney, stir and simmer until the kidney is tender, for approximately 5 minutes. Season and serve garnished with chopped parsley, and bread.

VEAL SWEETBREADS IN GARLIC AND OLIVE OIL

INGREDIENTS

1kg/2lb veal sweetbreads

60ml 2fl oz olive oil

50g/2oz butter

salt and pepper

2tsp garlic, crushed

1tbsp coriander or parsley, chopped

PREPARATION

≈ Prepare the sweetbreads: wash, blanch in boiling water for a couple of minutes, cool under the cold tap and then trim off any fatty or gristly bits.

≈ Remove the membranous skin, breaking off the nuggets of bread.

≈ Heat the oil and butter in a pan until hot.

≈ Toss the sweetbreads into the pan, season and stir over the heat for 5 minutes.

≈ Add the garlic and stir. Cook for a further couple of minutes.

≈ Add the chopped herbs.

≈ Tip into a warmed bowl and serve.

CHUNKED PORK IN ORANGE SAUCE

INGREDIENTS

¼ cup/50g/2oz butter or olive oil

1 small onion, finely sliced

¾ kg/1½lb pork fillet, cut into 2.5cm/1in cubes

grated rind of 2 oranges

juice of 3 oranges

⅝ cup/375ml/¾pt chicken stock (see Basic Recipes)

2 green chillies, chopped, or 2tsp chilli paste

1tsp garlic, crushed

1tbsp coriander or parsley, chopped

2tsp cornflour (cornstarch)

15ml/1tbsp cold water

salt and black pepper

PREPARATION

≈ In a large frying pan, heat the butter or oil.

≈ Sauté the onion until soft and golden, and remove from the pan.

≈ Add the pork to the pan and cook, stirring to brown all sides.

≈ Mix the orange rind, orange juice, stock, chilli, garlic and coriander or parsley together, and pour over the pork.

≈ Bring to the boil and add the onion slices. Simmer for 10 minutes.

≈ Remove the meat to a warm bowl.

≈ Mix the cornflour (cornstarch) with the water and add to the sauce to thicken it. Stir, season and pour over the meat.

CALDO GALLEGO SOUP

This is a lovely winter soup.

INGREDIENTS

50g/2oz butter
1 onion, chopped
½kg/1lb bacon, ham or pork knuckle
½tsp garlic, crushed
1 firm green cabbage (smallish), finely shredded
¾kg/1½lb potatoes, peeled and cut in pieces
10 cups/2l/4pt water
freshly ground black pepper

PREPARATION

NOTE: If using pork knuckle, simmer for 1½ hours first.

≈ In a large saucepan, melt the butter.

≈ Add the onion and cook gently until soft. Add the bacon and garlic.

≈ Add the cabbage and potato pieces, and cover for 5 minutes.

≈ Pour over the water. At this stage, add the pork knuckle (or cooked ham).

≈ Remove lid, grind over plenty of black pepper.

≈ Simmer for 1 hour. The soup should be thick; if you need to thicken, remove half the greens and potato and mash before returning to the pot.

≈ Season and serve in bowls, with crusty bread.

BAKED CHORIZO SAUSAGE

This delicious spicy sausage is now quite readily available in a number of supermarkets and delicatessens. It is a must for any tapas party.

PREPARATION

≈ Slice the sausage into rings, place in a hot oven (250°C/480°C/gas 9) and bake until just beginning to crisp around the edges. Serve with plenty of bread.

INDEX

Anchovy and mussels San
   Sebastián 38, **38**
anchovy potato salad 51, **51**
anchovy sauce 24
apricot sauce 89
artichoke hearts with tomato and
   lemon 61, **61**
asparagus and lettuce tarts 53,
   53
aubergine with cheese and
   prawns 68, **68**

Bacon and chicken with
   mussels 79
bacon-wrapped prawns with
   soured cream 18, **18**
baked chorizo sausage 93, **93**
beans:
   green 57, **57**
   kidney 60, **60**
   refried 60, **60**
blood sausage with tomato and
   garlic 87, **87**
bread 47
   garlic 47, **47**

Cabbage 64, **64**
calamares fritos 10
caldo Gallego soup 93, **93**
Carmona 58
ceviche of shrimp 17, **17**
cheese 70–1, **70–1**
cheese and potato croquettes 52,
   52
chicken 76–80, **76–80**
chicken in batter with honey and
   mustard 77, **77**
chicken empanada 79
chicken in garlic sauce 76, **76**
chicken livers with sherry
   vinegar 80
chicken stock 12
chilli king prawns 15, **15**
chilli manchego 71, **71**
chilli oil 11
chorizo sausage 93, **93**
chunked pork in orange sauce 92,
   92
cod 23, **23**
Córdoba 6, **28**
corn on the cob with garlic
   butter 49, **49**
courgettes 62–3, **62–3**
courgettes with dill 63, **63**
crab and brandy tartlets 21
cucumbers 54–5, **54–5**

Deep-fried whitebait 20, **20**
definitions 6–7
dips (see sauces)
drinks 7

Egg and garlic fried bread 74, **74**
eggplant (see aubergine)
empanadas 41, 79

Fish (see seafood)
fish croquettes 30
fish stock 12
fried sardines 22
fried squid 42, **42**
fried stuffed mussels 39, **39**

Galician stewed octopus 30, **30**
garlic bread 47, **47**
garlic mushrooms 48, **48**
garlic oil 11
garlic soup 46, **46**
garlic toast 27
gazpacho 38, 44, **44**
glazed king prawns 16, **16**
goat's cheese with tarragon and
   garlic marinade 70, **70**
green beans tapa 57, **57**

Ham 84, **84**
history 6

Ingredients 6, 7–10, 11–12

Jamón serrano 84, **84**

Kidneys in sherry sauce 90, **90**
king prawns (see prawns)

Lamb 88–9, **88–9**
lamb with apricot sauce 89, **89**
lobster and chicken brochettes 21

Marinated lamb cutlets 89, **89**
marinated whitebait 19, **19**
mayonnaise 11
meat 84–93
meatballs with garlic and
   tomato 88, **88**
Mediterranean vinaigrette 12
mint and chilli cucumber 55, **55**
monkfish with anchovy sauce 24,
   24
monkfish and bacon
   brochettes 26, **26**

monkfish Culiacin 24
mushrooms 48, **48**
mussel, shrimp and squid
   tapa 40, **40**
mussels 36–40, **36–40**
mussels and beans with
   tomato 36, **36**
mussels in gazpacho 38, **38**

Octopus 30–1, **30–1**
octopus with olive oil and
   paprika 31, **31**
oil:
   chilli 11
   garlic 11
olive oil (see oil)
olives 56, **56**
orange sauce 92
oysters Bloody Mary 33, **33**
oysters with lime 32, **32**

Paella croquettes 73, **73**
pastry:
   shortcrust 12
patatas bravas 49–50,
   49–50
peppers 65–7, **65–7**
pickled cucumbers with chilli 54,
   54
pork 92–3, **92–3**
potatoes 49–52, **49–52**
prawns 14–19, **14–19**, 40
prawns with egg and anchovy 18,
   18
prawns in garlic 14, **14**
prawns in garlic and herbs 19,
   19

Quail 82

Refried kidney beans 60, **60**
Ronda **7, 9**, 58

Salt cod with green peppers and
   potatoes **23**
sardines 22
sauces 22, 50
   anchovy 24
   apricot 89
   garlic 76
   orange 92
   sherry 90
   soured cream 18
   tomato 38
sausages 87, **87**, 93, **93**

scallops with lime and crab 34,
   34
scallops in tomato sauce 35
seafood 13–42
Seville **8, 10**, 58
sherry sauce 90
shortcrust pastry 12
shrimps (see prawns)
smoked fish mayonnaise and
   garlic toast 27, **27**
soups:
   caldo Gallego 93, **93**
   garlic 46, **46**
   gazpacho 38, 44, **44**
soured cream sauce 18
spinach and mussel pot 37, **37**
squid 40–2, **40, 42**
squid empanada 41
stewed giant olives 56, **56**
stock:
   chicken 12
   fish 12
stuffed cabbage leaves 64, **64**
stuffed chicken breasts 78
stuffed courgettes 62, **62**
stuffed green peppers with
   chilli 66, **66**
stuffed green peppers with
   hake 67, **67**
stuffed quail 82
stuffed tomatoes 45, **45**
sweetbreads 91, **91**

Three peppers in tomato and
   garlic 65, **65**
tomato salad with Mediterranean
   vinaigrette 44, **44**
tomato sauce 35
tomatoes 44–5, **44–5**
tortilla Española 72, **72**

Veal sweetbreads in garlic and
   olive oil 91, **91**
vegetables 44–68
vinaigrette:
   Mediterranean 12

Whitebait 19–20, **19–20**

Zucchini (see courgettes)